STUDY GUIDE TO ACCOMPANY
SULLIVAN • SHERMAN • HARRISON

A Short History of Western Civilization

EIGHTH EDITION

Volume One: to 1776

JOYCE E. SALISBURY

University of Wisconsin – Green Bay

McGraw-Hill, Inc.

New York   St. Louis   San Francisco   Auckland   Bogotá   Caracas   Lisbon
London   Madrid   Mexico City   Milan   Montreal   New Delhi
San Juan   Singapore   Sydney   Tokyo   Toronto

Study Guide to Accompany Sullivan-Sherman-Harrison:
A Short History of Western Civilization, Eighth Edition, Volume One: to 1776

This book is printed on recycled, acid-free paper containing a minimum
of 50% total recycled fiber with 10% postconsumer de-inked fiber.

1 2 3 4 5 6 7 8 9 0 DOC DOC 9 0 9 8 7 6 5 4

ISBN 0-07-026902-5

The editor was Sarah Touborg;
the production supervisor was Richard A. Ausburn.
R. R. Donnelley & Sons Company was printer and binder.

Cover credit: Limbourg Brothers, "Les Très Riches Heures du Duc de Berry, June," 1416,
Musée Condé, Chantilly. Giraudon/Art Resource.

CONTENTS

Map Exercises

INTRODUCTION

Welcome to the study of Western civilization. Often students at the beginning of their college careers feel a little overwhelmed by the amount of material to learn, even when it is interesting. I have designed this study guide to help you get the most from this course. Be aware that it is written not to help you memorize, but to help you think about what you are learning; to make it part of your experience. (In the process, of course, you will remember more of the material by using this method.) Furthermore, this guide will help teach you the techniques you need to approach such courses in the future, whether they are history courses or other courses in the humanities or social sciences. Good study skills are the same in many courses. Please read this introduction carefully, because it will tell you how to make the most of this study guide. Now, here's how to approach your course in Western civilization:

Read the Textbook

I know your professor has already told you this, but I want to add a few words about it. First, keep up with the reading. Read the required sections before each lecture; don't wait until just before the exam to try to read it all at once. You just won't absorb the material that way (nor will you enjoy it). Second, read effectively. Here are some suggestions on how to do that.

1. Understand the overall subject of the chapter *before* you start reading it closely. Do this by reading and rephrasing in your own words the chapter title and all the subheadings within the chapter. Then look at a map to find the areas you will be reading about to locate the region spatially. Finally, for the first few chapters, read the Overview section in this Study Guide before you start reading the chapter. (After you've practiced this for a few chapters, don't read the Overview until after you've read the chapter. I'll explain why below).

2. Read the chapter slowly and highlight or underline the main points. I mean the *main* points. If you are highlighting one-third of the page or more, you are doing too much and it won't help you when you go back and study. Some people recommend that you outline the chapter. If you have the time, that is of course very helpful. Most students tell me they do not have time to outline every chapter. If this is the case with you, then work on your highlighting technique; that is the most efficient way to use your time and convert the book into a study tool.

3. As you finish each section of a chapter, stop, put the book down, and summarize it in your own words. Then summarize the whole chapter in your own words. Don't worry about getting all the details; those will come later; just answer the general question, "What is this chapter about?" This is a very important skill, and you will get better with practice. Use the Overview in this Guide to check your summary of the chapter. Did you get the main points? Do not try to match my words; just be sure you've gotten the main points. It is most important to put your summary into your own words (just as I did when I wrote the Overview). You will find as the semester proceeds, you will get good at being able to summarize what you have read. Take this skill with you to all your courses (as well as to your work career later). It is a valuable skill, and good use of the Overview in the Study Guide will help you develop it.

4. Now turn to the Study Guide.

<u>Use the Study Guide</u>

The Study Guide is designed to help you do several things: 1) think about and assimilate the material you read in the chapter; 2) review the details of the chapter; 3) prepare you to take a test on the material; 4) remind you that each chapter is part of a whole picture by reviewing what went before and pointing to what is coming up. Each chapter of the Guide is divided into several sections, each designed to improve a particular skill. Here is how to use each section and an explanation of what each is intended to accomplish.

OVERVIEW

The Overview provides a short summary of each chapter. For the first few chapters, read this first to start to let you know what the chapter is about. After that, you should be able to orient yourself into a chapter by reading the main headings of the text before you start to read. Then use the Overview to check your own summary of the chapter. It will help you learn how to summarize the main points of what you have read.

MAP EXERCISE

It is almost impossible to figure out what is going on in history without a sense of where it is going on. Each time the textbook reaches a point where there is a geographic change, the Study Guide will include a blank map with questions. The questions are designed not only to help you remember *where* something is, but also to stimulate you to think about the importance of the location and relationship among things. The map exercises are designed to help you prepare for exams even if your professor does not include a map section on any given exam, so do not skip it.

STUDY QUESTIONS

Each chapter contains a list of study questions. These ask you to review the material in the chapter, but also to think about the material in new ways. Be sure always to support your general, theoretical answers with specific details. Not only will this give you practice formulating a convincing argument, but it will help you review the details within the chapter. Students often ask me how they can remember many of the details that are presented in a text. The answer is to put the details in contexts. (It's easier to remember the trees if you understand the layout of the forest.) As you work on these questions, you will be creating new contexts that will enclose the details you want to remember.

While you work on these study questions, do not just refer to the text looking for the answers. Many questions require you to synthesize material in the text and bring your ideas to it. That is what a good essay question on a test will do, so this will give you practice in that skill.

Each numbered Study Question usually has two to three questions within it. Don't be intimidated by this; it really isn't more questions. Listing multiple questions is simply a way to make sure you cover all the issues that are implicit in the first question. Therefore, the second and/or third questions urge you to elaborate on the first question. Treat each numbered Study Question as one topic. Listing several subquestions in this way is also designed to help you when you prepare for essay questions. Often essay questions are phrased as only one question, yet they virtually never require one easy phrase as an answer. Compound questions like these will help you get used to answering complex essay questions, and more importantly, practice thinking about issues in a many-faceted way.

Many of the Study Questions ask you to compare or contrast events with similar contemporary occurrences. These questions are important for many reasons, one of which is that you will remember things better if they connect to your experiences. Therefore, do not neglect these questions even if you know that your professor will not ask such questions on an exam. They are important learning tools.

The best way to work on Study Questions is in a small group. Try to put together a study group with other students in the class. Meet often and answer these questions together. Other people's insights might help you, and there is no better way to learn something than by explaining it to someone else. Students also tell me that discussing (and arguing) over ideas in such study groups has been one of the most rewarding elements of their Western civilization courses. And it improves their grades, too.

IDENTIFICATION

I have included a list of main people and events here as a reminder that you should have included all these items in your answers to the map exercises and study questions. As you read over this list, ask yourself (or better yet, ask each other as you work in a group) who or what the item was; when and where it lived, flourished, or took place; and what significance it had for the period under review. In this way, you can review your knowledge of these things and people. However, the most important way to remember these is not to memorize some fact about them, but to use them in context. Did you leave any out when you were answering the Study Questions and Map Exercise? If so, where would they fit in?

CHRONOLOGY

I have put an asterisk (*) by some of the people and events in the identification list. List these in chronological order. You will find that some of the items in the list happened at the same time. As you list these items, put a circle around those that are contemporary. This will give you an opportunity to review the chronology of events, and remind you which happened at the same time. This exercise will also give you a different context to consider the identification terms. It will help you remember them as well as help make sure you know the sequence of the main events.

SAMPLE QUESTIONS

Each chapter offers a list of sample questions that might appear on an objective examination. If you are in a small class and will be having essay exams, your work on the Study Questions has given you review for that sort of exam. What if you are in a large class, and have multiple choice exams? Of course, the material you have worked on has given you the knowledge you need to answer questions on an objective exam. All you lack is technique. Many students believe that multiple choice exams are easier than other kinds because the answer is there. All they have to do is find it. However, the main difficulty with such exams is that students often get themselves confused by the array of choices. The wrong answers on tests are called "distractors" and they do distract you from finding the correct answer. It would be misleading for me to give you sample multiple choice questions, because it would only get you used to the kind of distractors *I* write, which would not necessarily be the same kind written by your professor. So, the best way to prepare for a multiple choice exam is to practice techniques that will keep you from being confused by the distractors. Here's how to take an objective exam: 1) Read the question (not the answers). 2) Formulate an answer in your mind. 3) Find the answer that comes closest to the one you formulated. 4) Don't change your mind unless you have a really compelling reason.

Since that is the best way to take an objective exam, these Sample Questions are written as if they were objective questions, but without the distractors. Formulate the best answer. If you don't know, look it up (I've provided the page number so you can find it easily). Remember, these are only a few questions, so your test will have many more. All this section is doing is giving you some practice with this kind of question. You will have learned the content you need for objective exams by working through the Map Exercise and the Study Questions.

REVIEW AND ANTICIPATION

Each chapter in this guide closes with a few questions that urge you to think beyond the chapter you have been working on. These questions will tie each chapter's material to things that have gone before. These questions will also ask you to guess what might be coming up based on what you know. It does not matter whether you are right or wrong. What this does is give you further context that will make the subsequent chapters more meaningful (and thus easier to remember). It also lets you review previous material a little so it always stays part of your learning.

That's all there is to it. If you use this Study Guide as I've described, you will have all the tools you need to be successful in this course. You will also have learned valuable techniques that you can take to other courses. And I hope this Guide will help you relax and enjoy the learning of history. Good luck and have fun.

Chapter 1
The River Valley Civilizations:
Mesopotamia and Egypt, 4000-1750 B.C.

OVERVIEW

This chapter describes the growth and structures of human societies from the prehistoric Stone Age hunting and gathering peoples through the complex agricultural societies of ancient Mesopotamia and Egypt.

1. The Prehistoric Background. About 40,000 years ago, the human species evolved with the biological capacities that we define as human, including the ability to make and use tools. During the Old Stone Age (Paleolithic) period, societies lived by hunting and gathering. Slowly, societies developed leading to pastoral cultures of the Middle Stone Age (Mesolithic) and finally to the settled agricultural societies of the New Stone Age (Neolithic). Along with new technological innovations, agricultural societies brought new cultural and religious forms that were to shape future societies.

2. Mesopotamian Civilization: Political, Economic, and Social Life. Systematic irrigation of the land between the Tigris and Euphrates rivers permitted complex urban centers to grow where there had formerly been only small villages. The government of these city-states led to the institution of hierarchical organization, an established priesthood, writing, and a system of justice with written laws. There also arose the desire to build empires, larger political entities that would join smaller city-states together.

3. Mesopotamian Belief, Thought, and Expression. Impressive accomplishments in religion, literature, arts and sciences accompanied Mesopotamian political and economic advances. A complex polytheistic religion developed that had many rituals to assure fertility and appease the many gods and goddesses, but that offered little optimism for the individual. Their building, arts, literature and scientific advances grew out of people's religious inclinations.

4. Egyptian Civilization: Political, Economic, and Social Life. Egypt, too, developed a highly organized civilization based on the agriculture permitted by a huge river. This civilization was more centralized than that of Mesopotamia and through the varying fortunes of dynasties and periods of fluctuating stability, it was ruled by a powerful pharaoh, who was responsible for bringing order and justice to the people. A hierarchical social structure evolved based on the concept of the rule of a powerful individual and the organizing principle of an irrigation-based agricultural society.

5.   <u>Egyptian Belief, Thought, and Expression.</u> Early Egyptian civilization was noted for its cultural achievements, and most of these achievements grew out of people's strong religious beliefs. A polytheistic religion dominated all elements of their lives. A belief in an afterlife shaped their views of justice and contributed to impressive architecture (pyramids), hieroglyphic writings, and scientific accomplishments.

MAP EXERCISE

1.   Locate the Tigris, Euphrates and the Nile rivers on the map. Discuss why the rivers were important to the growth of these civilizations, and how they shaped the social structures of their respective civilizations.

2.   Locate Mesopotamia. Locate the Fertile Crescent. What portion of the Fertile Crescent is outside Mesopotamia and the Nile Valley? What features do all the parts of this area share that led it to be the "cradle of Western civilization"?

3.   Locate Palestine. Do you think this area would be vulnerable to conquest? Why or why not? From where would threats come?

4.   Locate the major cities of this area: Jerusalem, Babylon, Ur, Memphis, Akhetaton, Thebes, Troy. Which do you think would be most vulnerable to conquest? Why?

5.   Locate Asia Minor, Arabian Desert, Red Sea, Persian Gulf, Caucasus Mountains, and the Black Sea. Save all this geographic awareness for chapters to come (and for understanding the news).

STUDY QUESTIONS

1.   What types of economic activity characterized the Paleolithic and Neolithic periods? How did the social patterns and religious beliefs of each period reflect its economic characteristics?

2.   Describe the political structure of the Mesopotamian city-states, and discuss what elements contributed to their remarkable stability and prosperity. (Be sure to include all the structures that contributed to the political make-up including religion, writing, etc.)

3.   Describe the social structure of Mesopotamian society. What function did each group serve in society? (Include the position of women in your discussion.)

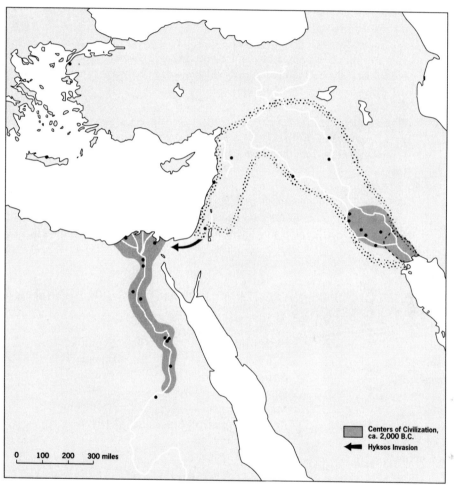

Centers of Civilization, ca. 2,000 B.C.

Hyksos Invasion

0   100   200   300 miles

MAP 1.1   Centers of the First Higher Civilizations: Mesopotamia and Egypt

4.   One of the features of settled societies is that they have to deal with the question of social justice. What was the concept of justice developed by Hammurabi, and what was the concept of justice developed in the Middle Kingdom of Egypt? Include in your discussion the relationship of justice to an afterlife. Which concept of justice is closest to our own? How?

5.   Describe Sumerian religious beliefs. Include their main deities, their rituals, literary and architectural expressions, and the prevailing feelings that emerged from such a religion.

6.   Describe the beginnings of empire-building in Mesopotamia. What forces contributed to the inclination to build empires, and what forces worked to delay the unification of this region?

7.   Discuss the scientific developments of the Sumerians and explain how those grew from their religious studies. Discuss the scientific achievements of the Egyptians. How was the pursuit of science in both these societies different from our own?

8.   Describe Egyptian religious beliefs. Include their main deities, the required rituals, literary, artistic and architectural expressions. How were the religious feelings of the Egyptians different from those of the Mesopotamians?

IDENTIFICATION

TRY TO USE EACH OF THESE TERMS AT LEAST ONCE IN ANSWERING THE STUDY QUESTIONS AND MAP EXERCISES

*Paleolithic	*Mesolithic	*Neolithic
Semitic	*Sargon I	*Hammurabi
cuneiform	pictogram	ziggurat
Hyksos	Isis	Amon
Ishtar	Marduk	hieroglyphic
ma'at	Epic of Gilgamesh	Osiris
*Old Kingdom	*Middle Kingdom	ka
Sumerian	Akkad	

CHRONOLOGY

List in chronological order the words in the Identification section that have an asterisk (*). As you list these items, put a circle around those that are contemporary.

SAMPLE QUESTIONS

1. What is the main feature that separates the Paleolithic and Mesolithic periods from the Neolithic? (pp. 4-7)

2. By 3100 B.C. what civilization had established itself in Mesopotamia based on an agricultural system dependent on irrigation? (p. 8)

3. What ancient king is known for his law code that, while brutal, attempted to bring the concept of justice to increasingly complex societies? (p. 10)

4. What culture first developed writing? (p. 11)

5. Who was the legendary king whose search for immortality formed the basis of a famous Mesopotamian religious epic? (p. 12)

6. During the Middle Kingdom, the pharaoh took on a special responsibility for the people. What was this responsibility? (p. 14)

7. What are some of the characteristics of Egyptian sculpture? (p. 17)

8. Why did Egyptians mummify dead bodies? (p. 15)

9. On what did the Egyptians devise their system of time reckoning? (p. 17)

REVIEW AND ANTICIPATION

1. Do you expect Egypt or Mesopotamia to remain free from foreign influence the longest? Why?

2. From what regions do you expect influence or conquest to come to these areas?

3. Are there any elements of the religious life of the peoples that we've studied that seem to be most vulnerable to (or open to) change?

Chapter 2
The Diffusion of Near Eastern
Civilization, 1750-800 B.C.

OVERVIEW

After 1750 B.C., the Near Eastern civilizations spread quickly. In addition, new influential cultures contributed to the complex mix that will become western culture.

1. Diffusion and the Movement of Peoples. The culture of the river civilizations spread by trade and war. Even more important in the spread of this culture was the movement of people into and near the civilized zones. Two especially important peoples in this process were the seminomadic peoples from the Arabian Desert and the Indo-Europeans from the north. These peoples adopted and transformed the cultures they found.

2. The Egyptian and Hittite Empires, 1750-1200 B.C. In 1558 B.C., Egypt established a rejuvenated "New Kingdom." Strong pharaohs engaged in a new policy of imperialism, spreading Egyptian control and culture into surrounding areas of Africa and into Palestine and Syria. This expansion confronted the expansion of the Hittites, who had established an empire in Asia Minor. Egypt was weakened internally by a religious struggle in which Akhnaton attempted to transfer worship to a new Sun God. After the old gods were restored, Egypt could turn again to its embattled empire. The Egyptians and Hittites finally agreed to divide the region into spheres of influence.

3. The Minoan World, 2000-1400 B.C. An advanced civilization developed on the island of Crete that influenced Greece and other civilizations. It was a society that had grown wealthy by trade and had developed technical and cultural advances. About 1450 B.C., the Minoan civilization was destroyed by natural disasters and invaders.

4. The Era of Small States, 1200-800 B.C.: Phoenicians and Arameans. The decline of the large empires allowed smaller states to prosper. Phoenicians and Arameans were both trading peoples who were prosperous and influential. The Phoenicians engaged in maritime trade throughout the Mediterranean world, and the Arameans were overland traders throughout the Near East and beyond. The Phoenician alphabet served as the model for subsequent written languages.

5. The Era of Small States, 1200-800 B.C.: The Hebrews. The Semitic Hebrews moved into the region from Egypt and unified the tribes forming

a strong state with the capital at Jerusalem. They were unique in the Middle East in their monotheistic religion which identified them as God's Chosen People. The small kingdom was conquered by various empires, and the Jewish peoples dispersed. However, their commitment to and identification with their own religion remained strong. Prophets further refined the moral and theological stand, and this small, dispersed population would ultimately exert a tremendous impact on western culture.

MAP EXERCISE

See map on p. 8.

1. Locate Egypt, Asia Minor, Arabia, Mesopotamia, Palestine, Greece, Crete, Phoenicia.

2. Locate the following cities: Thebes, Memphis, Babylon, Jerusalem, Mycenae, Knossos, Damascus, Troy.

3. Which is the Egyptian Empire? Which is the Hittite Empire? What region would likely be the area of most contention between these two peoples?

4. Where was the center of Minoan civilization? What was the capital? From where did the invaders come who destroyed the Minoan dominance of the region?

5. Mark a general route of the Hebrews as they moved from Egypt to Palestine to establish their state. Now mark how far they were taken when they were moved from Palestine to Babylon. Is it remarkable that they were able to retain their identity from all these distances?

STUDY QUESTIONS

1. What forces and peoples were significant in spreading the high civilization of the river valleys? *Semitic s emi nomads, Indo-Europeans*

2. The "New Kingdom" of Egypt was established with the goal of restoring old Egyptian life and values. How successful was this effort? What changes were introduced in Egyptian society? *the exaltation of the "divine ruler," cleansing" the land of the taint of foreigners, the return to the order in admin, economy, religion, and artitic + intellectual life.*

3. Describe the religious reform initiated by Akhnaton. Why wasn't it successful? *reestablish the phorahs absolute supremacy in the face of threats offered by such groups, military, royal officials + priests of Amon-RA / Attacks on other countries*

4. Describe Minoan government and economy. What helped this society prosper? What caused its downfall? *governed by several kings, each controlling a particular city and its surrounding territory; strong religious sanctions + on wealth derived from trade + agricultural. Royal administration was conducted by a highly developed bureaucracy especially skilled at records. / Economics = agricultural system + trade + industry produced additional wealth*

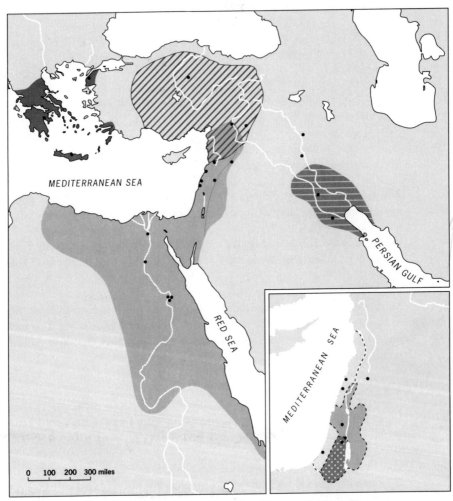

MAP 2.1 The Ancient Near East, ca. 1450 B.C.

5.   Contrast the mentality of the Minoan civilization with that of Mesopotamia and Egypt. What characteristics of Minoan outlook are revealed in their art and religion? *they all have worldly concerns, lacking in fear, open to experimenation, and pleasure loving decorated pottery, mobile art, energetic, integ*

6.   What small states were able to prosper with the disruption of the empires of Egypt and the Hittites? Which of these states benefited most by the decline of the Minoan civilization? *the Dhoenicians and the Arameans, / The Phoenicians*

7.   Describe the process by which the Hebrews changed from bands of nomads to an established unified kingdom. How long did this kingdom last? Who destroyed it? *worship one god / about a century the Philistine*

8.   Describe the religious ideas of the prophets of Israel as they refined people's understandings of the nature of God, humanity, and community. Which of these ideas do you think will have the greatest impact?

IDENTIFICATION

nature of God

TRY TO USE EACH OF THESE TERMS AT LEAST ONCE IN ANSWERING THE STUDY QUESTIONS AND MAP EXERCISES

Indo-European	*Hatshepsut	*Akhnaton
*Nefertiti	Aton	Amon-Ra
*Tutankhamon	Knossos	Linear A
Linear B	*Abraham	Yahweh
*exodus	*Solomon	diaspora
Torah	covenant	*David
*prophets		

CHRONOLOGY

List in chronological order the words in the Identification section that have an asterisk (*). As you list these items, put a circle around those that are contemporary.

SAMPLE QUESTIONS

1.   What permitted the less advanced Indo-European cultures to play an important political role in the Middle East? (p. 20) *the Nile River*

2.   What Egyptian influences spread throughout the Near East after the New Kingdom? (p. 22) *agricultural system*

3.   What pharaoh reintroduced the worship of Amon-Ra after the failure of Akhnaton's religious reforms? (p. 23) *Amenhotep IV*

4.   What was Linear B? (p. 24) *an early form of Greek language*

5.   In what trades were the Minoan craftsmen particularly skilled that allowed them to prosper from trade? (p. 25)

6.   What Minoan sport was featured in the artwork that seems to have been part of religious ritual? (p. 25) *life after death*

7.   What are some examples of advanced Minoan engineering? (p. 26) *building temples + palaces + tombs*

8.   What state replaced the Minoans as the most prosperous Mediterranean traders? (p. 26) *Phoenicians and the Arameans*

9.   Whose alphabet became the model for the written languages of the Mediterranean? (p. 26) *the Aramean language*

10.   What was the defining element in the Israelite identity? (p. 27)

11.   Who built the Temple in Jerusalem, and what was its significance? (p. 28) *Hebrews*

12.   What were the consequences of Hebrew belief in the "moral freedom" of individuals? (p. 30)

13.   What did the Jews expect of the Messiah? (p. 30) *wealth + endurance on the day of deliverance*

REVIEW AND ANTICIPATION

1.   Review the contributions of the river valley civilizations. Which do you see as having a continuing impact on these civilizations?

2.   What size states do you expect to be successful in the next chapters, small trading societies or larger empires? Why? Include in your discussion a consideration about how one might measure the "success" of a society.

Chapter 3
The Great Empires: Assyria and Persia, 800-300 B.C.

OVERVIEW

The previous millennium had seen the spread of river valley cultures so that the region shared many cultural, economic and religious interests. Now powers would arise that would unify the region politically and attempt to maintain larger units than had previously been sustained.

1. The Assyrian Empire, 800-612 B.C. The Assyrians built a strong military force, pursued a policy of terrorism and conquered Mesopotamia, Palestine and Egypt. They collected tribute from this large area and governed with brutality. Their rule stimulated trade and the exchange of ideas throughout the region. Kings used their wealth to build huge monuments and construct a library that preserved many cultural traditions. Neighboring groups finally brought down the dreaded empire.

2. Successors of Assyria, 612-550 B.C. After the fall of the Assyrian Empire, several states tried to become the dominant power in the region. A restored Egypt under the twenty-sixth dynasty attempted to reestablish its empire, but reliance on foreign mercenaries and a reactionary priesthood impeded their efforts. Lydia and Media, too, were prosperous and strong, but neither was a match for the strength of the Persians. Most impressive was the kingdom of the Chaldeans, centered on the magnificent city of Babylon. The Chaldeans conquered the Hebrews and moved the people to Babylon. They built a great cultural center, but even their power was not equal to that of the Persians.

3. The Persian Empire, 550-330 B.C. Cyrus began the Persian expansion that was to culminate in the largest empire yet seen in this region. The Persians governed efficiently, building an effective bureaucracy with a good communication system. Furthermore, they governed with a policy of tolerance that made their rule benign. One of the influential aspects of the Persian rule was the new religion Zoroastrianism, which interpreted the world as a cosmic struggle between opposing principles of good and evil. This system encouraged individuals to seek moral perfection in their actions.

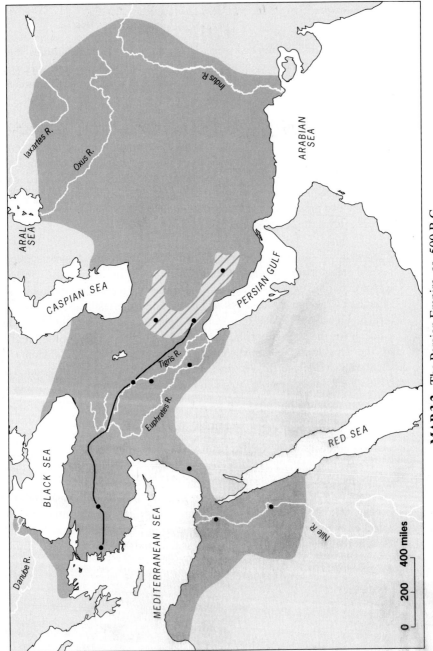

MAP 3.2 The Persian Empire, ca. 500 B.C.

MAP EXERCISE

1.   Locate Arabia, Egypt, India, Greece, Macedonia, Lydia.

2.   Locate the following cities: Nineveh, Sardis, Ecbatana, Susa, Persepolis. Which city do you think would make the most effective capital for the Assyrian Empire? Why? Would the same city be effective for the Persian Empire?

3.   Draw a line on this map that indicates the extent of the Assyrian Empire. Circle the Assyrian homeland.

4.   Locate the Persian homeland on this map. Note the extent of the Persian Empire. With which land do you expect Persia to come into most immediate conflict?

STUDY QUESTIONS

pg 33
pg 19

1.   Describe the organization and operation of the Assyrian Empire. What contributed to its downfall? *well-armed infantrymen, archers, + charioteers, skilled engineers • deliberate terorism / undying desire Constant warfare, threat of absorption + greed for the empire*

2.   What contributions did the Assyrians make to the history of the region? Which do you think will be the most enduring? *to erect a centralized monarchy, peace on the Near East, promoted trade by breaking down barriers, spread of common language, literary activities, religion*

3.   Which of the successors of Assyria before the rise of Persia seemed the strongest and most likely to replace the Assyrian Empire? Why? What prevented these states from building a large empire? *the Chaldeans played a major in destroying the Assyrians Empire / Syria + Palestine were conquered / weak economic + military strengths*

4.   Describe the system of government established by the Persians. What elements made this an efficient system? What caused it some instability? *Central authority divided into twenty large districts, records of accounts / often exploitation*

5.   Contrast the treatment toward subject peoples shown by the Assyrians and the Persians. Which do you think was shown to be most effective in the long run. Why?

Persians

6.   Explain the religious system of Zoroaster. What is the main difference between this system and that of the Hebrews? How were followers of Zoroastrianism supposed to behave? Why? *Set up a system based on dualism / good god Ahura Mazda Bad god Ahriman live by moral perfection by acting and thinking according to right*

pg 40

IDENTIFICATION

TRY TO USE EACH OF THESE TERMS AT LEAST ONCE IN ANSWERING THE STUDY QUESTIONS AND MAP EXERCISES

*Sargon II	*Ashurbanipal	Aramaic
Assur	Marduk	*Nebuchadnezzar II
Croesus	*Cyrus	*Darius I
Immortals	satrapies	satrap
Zoroaster	*Zoroastrianism	Ahura Mazda

CHRONOLOGY

List in chronological order the words in the Identification section that have an asterisk (*). As you list these items, put a circle around those that are contemporary.

SAMPLE QUESTIONS

1. Assyrian military successes increased after they adopted what military innovations? (p. 33)   archry, charateers

2. What policy adopted to maintain order in its empire marked the rule of the Assyrians? (p. 34)   monarchy

3. What common spoken language did the Assyrians spread over their empire? (p. 34)   Aramaic

4. What prevented the Egyptians from recapturing their empire after the fall of Assyria? (p. 36)   the chaldeans

5. What impact did the Chaldean conquest of Jerusalem have on the Hebrew people? (p. 36)   they were deported to Babylon as captives

6. In what city was the legendary Tower of Babel? (p. 36)   Babylon

7. Who was the famous principle god of the Chaldeans? (p. 36)   Yahweh

8. What king permitted the Hebrews to return from their Babylonian captivity and rebuild the Temple? (p. 38)   Darius I

9. What was the Persian system of satrapies? (p. 39)   twenty large districts

10. What did Zoroaster see as the fundamental principle in the cosmic order? (p. 40)   the principle dualism

11.   Who eventually conquered the Persian Empire? (p. 41)

    Assyrians

REVIEW AND ANTICIPATION

1.   What military innovations had the Hittites introduced? How did the Assyrians use these?

2.   The Egyptians had been successful establishing a divine kingship. Compare their kingship with that of the Assyrians and Persians. Which kind of kingship would make the most effective governing tool?

3.   What elements of the great empire established by the Persians will serve as an enticing model for other conquerors?

Chapter 4
The Origins and Development of the Greek
City-State Polity

OVERVIEW

A remarkable civilization grew on the Greek peninsula, a land dominated by mountainous terrain that worked against political unity, poor soil that precluded easy prosperity, and proximity to the sea that spurred trading. The origins of this civilization lay in the Mycenaean past, but the real formation lay in the development of the city-states that dominated the Golden Age.

1. The Mycenaean and Dark Ages, 2000-800 B.C.: Greek Origins. The earliest society we can identify on the Greek mainland is called the Mycenaean. It was a highly developed society, dominated by powerful warlords who built large fortresses. In about 1200 B.C., this society collapsed. In the subsequent "Dark Ages" of Greek society, people were no longer literate, and society retreated to small-scale agriculture. Yet, during this time, small communities developed that formed the basis for the greatness that was to come.

2. The Greek Archaic Age, 800-500 B.C.: Development of the *Polis*. During the Archaic Age, Greek city-states developed in ways that helped the citizens feel a close sense of community. The cities organized around a central fortress that provided a focal point for civic loyalty. Cities developed citizen armies. Greek colonies spread the city-state structure all over the Mediterranean. Finally, political reform led to democracy being established in many city-states, completing the process by which citizens took responsibility for their cities.

3. Athens. Like many city-states, Athens progressed through stages leading finally to democracy. At first leadership was vested in a king and noble clan heads. Slowly reformers like Solon worked to address some of the abuses of the nobles, but that was not enough to save the form of government. Tyrants ruled, further breaking the power of the nobility. Finally, Cleisthenes and Pericles reorganized society into territorial units of citizens (males over 18), and made other reforms to allow citizens to participate fully in the democratic running of the city-state.

4. Sparta. Sparta developed a different system from the other city-states. After conquering the local populace and fearing revolt, Sparta organized itself into a military state. Spartan men devoted their lives to the military, and the other work was done by slaves or noncitizens.

5.   <u>The Character of the *Polis*.</u> Greek city-states were small entities within which residents interacted intimately. Within this setting, male citizens were actively involved in a political process and setting that nourished both fierce patriotism and a high level of individual achievement.

MAP EXERCISE

See Map on p. 18.

1.   Locate the following: Iberia, Gaul, Sicily, Greece, Crete, Cyprus, Egypt, Ionia, Crimea, Black Sea, Atlantic Ocean.

2.   Locate the following cities: Rome, Syracuse, Carthage, Tyre.

3.   Shade the areas of Greek colonization. Which area represented the first colonies?

4.   Shade the areas of Phoenician colonization. In what regions do you expect Greek interests and Phoenician interests to conflict?

STUDY QUESTIONS

1.   Describe Mycenaean society. How did it develop, and how did it collapse? What skills were lost to Greece after the fall of the Mycenaeans?

2.   Describe Greek society during the Dark Ages. What important structures that were formed during that time shaped the future of Greece?

3.   Describe the urban space that shaped the character of the *polis*. What were the main elements and how would each contribute to building a sense of community among the citizens?

4.   What changes in Greek warfare took place between the Dark Age and the Archaic Age? How did these changes increase people's loyalty and attachment to the *polis*?

5.   Describe the process by which many city-states moved from oligarchy to democracy. How did Athens move through these stages?

6.   What reforms did Solon make? What group of people was he trying to help? To what degree were his reforms successful?

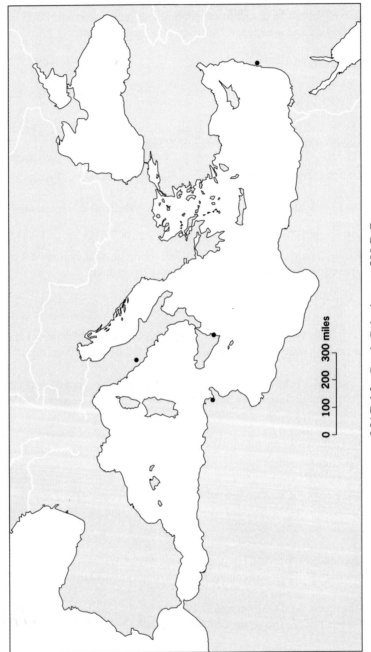

MAP 4.2 Greek Colonies, ca. 500 B.C.

0   100   200   300 miles

7.   Describe the form of democracy in Athens as it had been established by the time of Pericles. What features increased the level of participation? Who was left out of democratic participation?

8.   Describe the way of life of the Spartans. What values did they hold? How did this way of life grow out of their conquest of the Messenians?

9.   What social groups made up Spartan society? Which had the most freedom in their lives?

10.   Discuss the strengths and weaknesses of the city-state form of government in general. What kinds of feelings did this form generate in its citizens; what kinds of accomplishments?

IDENTIFICATION

TRY TO USE EACH OF THESE TERMS AT LEAST ONCE IN ANSWERING THE STUDY QUESTIONS

*Minoans	*Mycenaean	*Homer
*Dark Ages	Hellenes	acropolis
agora	oligarchy	phalanx
hoplites	tyrant	democracy
polis	Areopagus	Cleisthenes
Solon	*demes*	*helots*
Pericles	Lycurgus	Hesiod
perioeci	*Trojan War	Council of 500
archons	*gerousia*	

CHRONOLOGY

List in chronological order the words in the Identification section that have an asterisk (*). As you list these items, put a circle around those that are contemporary.

SAMPLE QUESTIONS

1.   What is the evidence for the warlike character of Mycenaean society? (p. 45)

2.   What probably caused the fall of Mycenaean culture? (p. 45)

3.   What elements of Mycenaean culture were lost during the "Dark Ages"? (p. 46)

4.   From where did the Greeks learn a new alphabet to replace the Linear B script? (p. 46)

5.   What early elements of democracy were visible in the Dark Age Greek communities? (p. 46)

6.   What is the significance of the *acropolis* for the Greek city-states? (p. 47)

7.   What were the regions of Greek colonization during the Archaic Age? (p. 49)

8.   What were the forces that brought about democracy in many of the Greek city-states? (pp. 50-51)

9.   What kind of agricultural reform did Solon introduce in Athens? (p. 52)

10.   What reforms did Pericles introduce to increase the participation of more citizens in the democratic process? (p. 54)

11.   In the Spartan system of government, who held power? (p. 56)

12.   What characteristics did all Greek city-states share? (p. 56)

13.   What was it about city-state life that encouraged individual achievement? (p. 57)

REVIEW AND ANTICIPATION

1.   Review the characteristics of Minoan culture. What elements did Mycenaean culture share with Minoan? What economic characteristic did Greek city-states in general share with the Minoan?

2.   What strengths and weaknesses of the democratic system as established in Athens do you think will emerge? Do you think this system will permit growth into a larger political unit than the city-state?

3.   Given the relative strengths and weaknesses of the two systems of Athens and Sparta, in a war between the two, who do you think would win?

Chapter 5
The Greek Golden Age, 500-336 B.C.:
Life, War, and Politics

OVERVIEW

Daily life in the Greek *poleis* stimulated individual accomplishment. However, except under threat of foreign invaders, these city-states were fiercely competitive. This led to wars among the city-states and ultimately conquest by Macedonia.

1. Daily Life in Greece. The daily life in Greek city-states for men was dominated by the public life of the *polis*. Most of the work (agricultural and manufacturing) involved small-scale production, and much of it was done by slaves and foreigners. This left male citizens a good deal of leisure time. It was spent in company and discourse with other men. Greek women were largely confined to the home and even there were withdrawn from the company of male visitors. Women could own no property, nor participate in political life.

2. The Persian Wars, 490-479 B.C. In response to rebellions by Greeks in Asia Minor, the Persians invaded the Greek mainland. Uncharacteristically, the Greek city-states aligned with each other to repel the invaders. They were successful by combining Sparta's strong army with Athens' skillful navy.

3. The Delian League and the Athenian Empire, 479-431 B.C. The Delian League was an alliance of many city-states that was established to prevent any further Persian threat. Members contributed ships and money, and Athens provided the leadership. It was successful at first, but soon Athens converted the League to an empire, in which the individual liberty of the other states was restricted, and the money contributed for military defenses was used for Athens' benefit.

4. The Peloponnesian War, 431-404 B.C. The Spartan-led Peloponnesian League went to war against Athens to stop Athenian expansion. Since Athens relied on its navy and Sparta its infantry, the war dragged on for years. Finally, with Persian naval support and rebellion of Athens' allies, Sparta was victorious. The leadership of Athens was brought to an end.

5. The Twilight of the World of the Greek City-States, 404-336 B.C. During the seventy years after the Peloponnesian War, the Greek city-states devoted many human and material resources on a series of wars in which one city-state tried to exert hegemony over the others. None was able to work out a

political path to unity. This fierce loyalty to one's city-state brought an end to the high point of Greek civilization.

6.   The Macedonian Conquest of Greece. Philip II of Macedon took advantage of the instability in the Greek city-states to establish control over the peninsula. He imposed a mild peace that offered the Greek city-states a way to end their incessant warfare, and to join him against their old enemy, Persia.

MAP EXERCISE

1.   Locate Athens, Sparta, Macedonia, Delos, Corinth, Miletus, the Hellespont, and the Persian Empire.

2.   From what direction did the Persians invade Greece? How would the Persian army have been supplied? Why were the naval victories so crucial for the Greeks?

3.   In the shaded areas, note which were Athens and its allies during the Peloponnesian war, which were Sparta and its allies, and which were neutral. Given these locations, what would have been the advantage of each side? Was there anything about the location of the neutral states that made it easier for them to remain neutral?

4.   Is Macedonia conveniently located to conquer Greece? Why? Is it conveniently located to conquer anywhere else?

STUDY QUESTIONS

1.   Describe the social structure of the Greek *polis*. Include a description of the various classes and of the economic life that made up the basis of the society.

2.   Contrast the daily lives of men and women. (Include in your discussion Thucydides' description of elements of daily life [p. 67].) What were the responsibilities of each? From whom did each get companionship? *from the polis*

3.   During the Archaic Age, what kinds of things encouraged interdependence among the Greeks? *Common language , religion , athlethic competition.*

4.   What strategy did the Spartans and Athenians use in withstanding the threat of the Persians? What were the significant battles of the war? Who won?

5.   What were the initial goals of the Delian League? Were they successful?

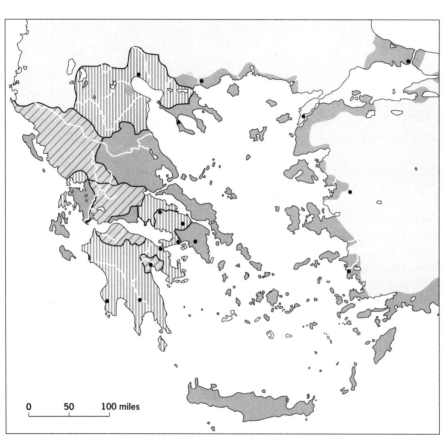

MAP 5.2 The Greek World, 431 B.C.

6. What steps did Athens take to convert the Delian League into an empire for its own benefit? Were Athenian actions consistent with Thucydides' description (p. 67) of Athenian morality?

7. What were the respective military strategies of Athens and Sparta in the Peloponnesian war? Why didn't the Athenians abide by the Fifty-Year Truce that was agreed to in 422 B.C.? What was the result of the war?

   Social + cultural = difference , imperalism
   Economic factor of trade

8. What city-states struggled for power after the Peloponnesian War? Were any of them able to unify Greece? Why wasn't Sparta able to sustain its leadership?

9. Describe the terms of the League of Corinth imposed by Philip II of Macedon. Did these terms offer a reasonable solution to the Greek instability?

IDENTIFICATION

Polis (City-state)

TRY TO USE EACH OF THESE TERMS AT LEAST ONCE IN ANSWERING THE STUDY QUESTIONS AND MAP EXERCISES

Aspasia	Pericles	*phratry*
gymnasia	*Darius	*Xerxes
*Marathon	Themistocles	*Thermopylae
*Delian League	*Thirty Years'	*Fifty-Year Truce
*Alcibiades	Truce	*Lysander
*Philip II	*League of Corinth	Hellenic League
Peloponnesian		
League		

CHRONOLOGY

List in chronological order the words in the Identification section that have an asterisk (*). As you list these items, put a circle around those that are contemporary.

SAMPLE QUESTIONS

1. What kinds of products were produced on the most productive Greek farms? (p. 59)

2. How did the ancient Greeks control the number of children they had? (p. 60)

3. What was the prime role for respectable Greek women? (p. 60)

4. What activities took place at the *gymnasia*, and why were they central to the life of the *polis*? (pp. 60-1)

5. What triggered the Persian invasion of Greece? (p. 61)

6. The Athenian leader Themistocles invested in what form of defense for the Athenians that was to have long-range implications for Athenian strategy? (p. 63)

7. What spheres of influence were decided upon by Athens and Sparta in the Thirty Years' Truce of 445 B.C.? (p. 64)

8. What did Athens use the Delian League "tribute" money for once the Persian threat was over? (p. 64)

9. Being subject to Athens increased the security and commerce of the city-states, so why did they object so strongly to Athenian rule? (p. 65)

10. What city-state is usually given responsibility for causing the devastating Peloponnesian War? Why? (p. 66)

11. What was the result of the Peloponnesian War for Athens? (p. 66)

12. How was the power of Sparta crushed? (p. 68)

13. What motivated Philip II of Macedon to become involved in Greece? (p. 68)

14. What did Philip II require of the defeated Greeks? (p. 69)

REVIEW AND ANTICIPATION

1. Review the description of Athenian democracy in the previous chapter. Does Thucydides' description of Athenian life seem an accurate summary?

2. Review the description of life in Sparta. What elements of the structure established there by Lycurgus contributed to its downfall in the fourth century B.C.?

3. Do you expect the fairly loose League of Corinth to be sufficiently stable to allow the Greek city-states to continue to be relatively independent? Or, do you expect another strong empire to conquer the city-states?

Chapter 6
Greek Thought and Expression

OVERVIEW

The Greek society of the *polis* generated a cultural achievement in virtually all fields that left an enduring impact on western culture. The Greeks studied the human condition and gained insights into truth and beauty that remain meaningful.

1.   Religion. Greek religion permeated all aspects of Greek life and provided a stimulus to artistic production. The Greeks believed in a pantheon of gods who resembled human beings and interfered in human affairs. Their world was also shaped by abstract forces such as fate and justice, and populated by many spirits. Greek emotional needs were filled by passionate mystery religions like the cult of Dionysus. Religious activities included honoring the gods with almost every kind of human activity, from sports events to the arts, and the civic cults formed an important part of the life of the city-states.

2.   Literature. Greek explorations of the human condition and human motivations yielded great literature. The earliest portrayals of heroic behavior were Homer's epics. Lyric poets framed human feeling. Perhaps most enduring were the dramatists of tragedies who explored human actions in the face of fate. Comic dramatists satirized politics and society. Most famous of the prose literature was that of the historians, who struggled to find truth about the past and have it illuminate the present.

3.   Art. Greek architects developed beautiful public buildings in a rectangular ground plan dominated by columns. These buildings reflected the ideals of proportion and balance. The temples on the Acropolis of Athens demonstrate these principles. Sculptors adorned the buildings and portrayed idealized human figures that reflected the power and potential of human beings.

4.   Philosophy and Science. Greek philosophers challenged traditional beliefs in mythological explanations and introduced an understanding of the world that was based on rational analysis. Some thinkers sought to understand the nature of the universe, finding materialistic or nonmaterialistic explanations. Some of the most influential thinkers focused on the place of human action in the world. Socrates established a method for deriving universal truths, and his student Plato developed his method into an analysis of ideal forms as reality. Aristotle believed that an ideal form could not exist outside the material world so he turned people's attention to the world itself. Hippocrates created a new approach that separated medicine from superstition.

5.   The Greek Spirit. Certain aspects of the Greek spirit have made a great impact on western culture. Greek thought that emphasized humanity and rationalism continues to exert a great influence. However, Greek society was more complex than that. It included much that was elitist and exclusive.

STUDY QUESTIONS

1.   How did the Greek religion encourage artistic production? Did the nature of the gods and goddesses themselves also serve to praise human achievement? How?

2.   Describe the elements of a mystery religion. Why would this have appealed to people? Do you think this form of religion might still appeal?

3.   What was the ideal behavior portrayed by Homer's heroes? How was this ideal expressed in the dramas of Aeschylus and Sophocles?

4.   Who were the Greek historians, and what were they trying to do in their works?

5.   What were the elements that characterized Greek architecture? Include in your discussion an analysis of the illustrations in Figure 4.1 (Chapter 4) and 6.2. How does this architecture mirror elements that Greek philosophers found important?

6.   How did Greek sculptors portray the human figure? Why? Include in your discussion Figure 5.1 (Chapter 5), 6.1 and 6.3. How does this sculpture mirror elements that Greek dramatists found important?

7.   Contrast the views of Plato and Aristotle on the nature of ultimate reality. Which one derives most from the nonmaterialist philosophical tradition? Which comes closest to our scientific view?

8.   Describe the perfect state as outlined by Plato in the *Republic*. Would you agree with him that this is the perfect governmental form?

9.   What innovations did Hippocrates make in approaching medicine?

10.   "Greek thought was intensely humanistic and rationalistic." Explain this statement and use evidence from religion, literature, art and philosophy to support your analysis.

IDENTIFICATION

TRY TO USE EACH OF THESE TERMS AT LEAST ONCE IN ANSWERING
THE STUDY QUESTIONS

Zeus	Athena	Dionysus
*Homer	*Iliad*	*Odyssey*
*Hesiod	*Sappho	Pindar of Thebes
*Aeschylus	*Sophocles	*Euripides
*Aristophanes	*Herodotus	*Thucydides
acropolis	Parthenon	Praxiteles
Democritus	*Socrates	sophists
*Plato	*Aristotle	*Hippocrates
Achilles	Helen	Odysseus
hubris	*Pythagoras	

CHRONOLOGY

List in chronological order the words in the Identification section that have an asterisk
(*). As you list these items, put a circle around those that are contemporary.

SAMPLE QUESTIONS

1.   For the Greeks, what were two of the abstracted forces that provided the
order for governing the universe? (p. 72)

2.   Why did the Olympic Games develop? (p. 73)

3.   What was the significance of oracles for the Greek people, and where was
the most famous one? (p. 73)

4.   What kind of religious cult satisfied people's personal emotional needs and
helped to provide mystic experiences? (p. 73)

5.   What was the setting of Homer's epic, the *Iliad*? (p. 74)

6.   Who was the famous poetess of Lesbos, and what themes did she explore in
her poetry? (p. 74)

7.   What was Oedipus' inadvertent crime as portrayed in the play by Sophocles?
(p. 75)

8.   Describe the two kinds of columns found on the Acropolis. (p. 76)

9.   What were the dominant traits of Greek sculpture and painting? (p. 77)

10. What feature most sharply distinguished Greek thought from that of earlier civilizations? (p. 78)

11. What was the materialistic explanation of the nature of the universe, and who was one of its proponents? (pp. 78-9)

12. What was the Socratic method? (p. 79)

13. What did Plato argue was the fundamental reality of the universe? (p. 80)

14. What did Aristotle say was necessary for people to achieve happiness? (p. 81)

15. How did Socrates die? (p. 79)

REVIEW AND ANTICIPATION

1.   Review the selection on the Peloponnesian War by Thucydides in the previous chapter. Do you think that selection reveals the objective truth that the historian was striving for?

2.   Reflection upon the great truths of the universe and the human experience grew out of the political life of the *polis*. Do you think such reflection will continue when that form of political life is ended by the conquest of Alexander?

Chapter 7
Greek Imperialism:
The Hellenistic World, 336-31 B.C.

OVERVIEW

The conquests of Alexander the Great spread Hellenic culture to a wide area in Asia and Africa. This culture mixed with Near Eastern civilization is called "Hellenistic" and formed its own characteristics.

1. Alexander the Great. Alexander was 20 years old when his father died, and he continued his father's plan to attack the Persian Empire. His conquests were brilliant, and he not only conquered the empire, but he continued into India. He died at the age of 33, leaving a vast empire, little plan for its governance, and a legend that would profoundly influence subsequent generations.

2. Hellenistic Political Developments. Alexander's empire broke up into three main kingdoms established by three of his companions. These states were ruled by monarchs who depended upon the support of Greek city-states established within their borders. Each state had its own particular problems and a tenuous balance of power was established among them until the growing Roman power eventually took them over.

3. Hellenistic Economic and Social Life. The economic impact of the Greek-Macedonian expansion was not great. Traditional forms of agriculture remained the rule and new technological advances were not forthcoming. Trade increased, making some areas more prosperous, particularly in Egypt, Syria, and Asia Minor. The gap between rich and poor increased dramatically, creating more social tensions than had existed in the *polis*.

4. Hellenistic Thought and Expression. As Greek culture expanded to the east, transformations occurred in traditional Hellenic ideas. Literary output was spurred by a highly literate public and wealthy patronage. However, much of it was unoriginal and derivative of classical Greek literature. Hellenistic art was transformed, showing increased realism and emotionalism that had been absent from classical works. The largest advances were in science and philosophy. Scientists made great discoveries in geography, mathematics, and medicine. Philosophers turned from the large subjects that had preoccupied Plato, and focused on how the individual could live a good life.

5. Hellenistic Religion. Mystery religions became increasingly popular in the Hellenistic world, and their spread led to a mingling of various religions that pointed toward the emergence of a common faith. Judaism, too, was

somewhat affected by the Hellenistic culture. Many Jews were "Hellenized," but the Maccabean Revolt showed that Jews would fight to keep their traditional way of life.

MAP EXERCISE

See map on p. 32.

1. Locate the following bodies of water: Mediterranean Sea, Black Sea, Caspian Sea, Red Sea, Persian Gulf. All these have been significant in the developing culture of this region.

2. Locate the following: India, Indus River, Arabian Desert, Mesopotamia, Egypt, Macedonia, Greece.

3. Where did Alexander make his initial campaigns against the Persian Empire? Why was that strategically a good idea?

4. Notice the three main Hellenistic states that remained after the breakup of Alexander's empire. Which of the three do you think will be most stable? Which least? Why?

STUDY QUESTIONS

1. Contrast the situation of the three Hellenistic monarchies that were established after the death of Alexander. What particular problems did each face? What ultimately happened to them?

2. What happened to the Greek city-states after their conquest by Macedonia? Did they stop the intercity intrigue that had brought about their conquest?

3. Hellenistic politics represented an uneasy balance between free city-states and eastern-style monarchies. Explain this balance and why each supported the other.

4. Describe the economic life of the Hellenistic cities. What elements remained essentially the same as before the Macedonian conquest, and what changed?

5. Describe Hellenistic art. What was similar to the Hellenic art and what was different? Contrast Figure 7.2 with Figure 6.3 in your discussion.

6. Why did Alexandria become a center for scientific inquiry? Describe some of the developments in science that occurred there. Which do you think has the most important impact?

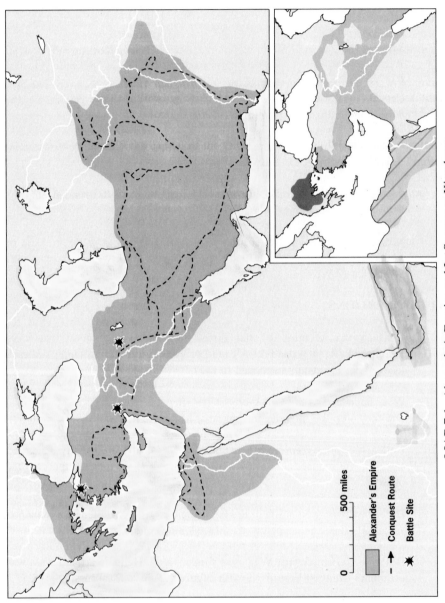

MAP 7.1 Alexander's Empire and Its Successor Kingdoms

500 miles

Alexander's Empire

Conquest Route

Battle Site

0

7.   What were the main preoccupations of Hellenistic philosophy? What were the main schools of thought? Compare and contrast them.

8.   What were the main elements of mystery religions? How did the popularity of these religions lead to religious syncretism in the Hellenistic world?

9.   How was Judaism affected by the occupation of the Hellenistic monarchies? What tensions were created within Judaism, and what evidence is there that they maintained old traditions?

IDENTIFICATION

TRY TO USE EACH OF THESE TERMS AT LEAST ONCE IN ANSWERING THE STUDY QUESTIONS AND MAP EXERCISES

Alexander	Darius III	Antigonid kingdom
Seleucid kingdom	Ptolemaic kingdom	Aetolian League
Achaean League	*Venus de Milo*	Euclid
Hipparchus	Archimedes	Skeptics
Cynics	Epicurus	Stoicism
Zeno	*apatheia*	syncretism
Septuagint	Maccabean Revolt	

SAMPLE QUESTIONS

1.   How far eastward did Alexander conquer? (p. 85)

2.   What style of rulership did Alexander create that was inconsistent with Greek and Macedonian tradition? (p. 85)

3.   What was the chief preoccupation of the Macedonian monarchy? (p. 87)

4.   Why was the Ptolemaic state the most stable of the Hellenistic states? (p. 87)

5.   What was the basis for the king's power in the Hellenistic monarchies? (p. 88)

6.   What was the main source of wealth in the Hellenistic world? (p. 89)

7.   How did opportunities for women change in the Hellenistic cities from the old Greek *polis*? (p. 90)

8.   What cities were the new cultural centers of the Hellenistic world? Which was particularly known for scientific advances? (p. 90, 92)

9.   What new characteristics dominated Hellenistic sculpture? (p. 91)

10.   What were some advances in mathematics made during the Hellenistic period? (p. 93)

11.   Why was daily life during the Hellenistic era little affected by the advances in science? (p. 93)

12.   What did Epicurus say humans should occupy themselves with? (p. 94)

13.   What did the Stoics mean by *apatheia*? (p. 94)

14.   What helped mystery religions appeal to people of all classes? (p. 95)

15.   What was the Septuagint, and why was it created? (p. 96)

REVIEW AND ANTICIPATION

1.   Review the life of the *polis* of traditional Greece. What elements were lost during the Hellenistic world? Could democracy have worked in the Hellenistic cities?

2.   Review the Persian administration of their empire. What elements were maintained by the Hellenistic rulers?

3.   What are the main sources of tension in the Hellenistic world? Do you think those same sources will remain after the conquest by Rome?

4.   What elements of mystery religions do you think will make their followers convert readily to Christianity?

Chapter 8
The Rise of Rome to Domination of the
Mediterranean World, 800 B.C.-133 B.C.

OVERVIEW

During these centuries, Rome created a political order that spread elements of Hellenic culture throughout the Mediterranean world. This accomplishment built upon a solid social order in Rome and spread slowly through conquest.

1. The Origins of Rome to 509 B.C. The early Indo-European settlers in the center of the Italian peninsula were favored with good geographical factors and exposure to Greeks and Etruscans who contributed much to their growing civilization. The new city-state of Rome was made up of two classes of people and ruled by a king, who was advised by a council. In 509 B.C., the Romans dethroned the Etruscan king and established a republic, ruled by two *consuls* elected annually and the patrician leaders of the Senate.

2. The Early Republic, 509-265 B.C. During the early centuries of the republic, Rome fought a long succession of wars against the surrounding tribes. Military successes combined with generous treatment of conquered peoples allowed Rome to control the Italian peninsula. Internally, Rome reshaped its political structures to allow the two classes, patricians and plebeians, to share political power, thus increasing the loyalty of its citizens. In spite of changes, however, Roman culture was conservative, dominated by values of home (with the father as sole head), farm, warfare, and religion. These values and a respect for tradition dominated Roman life throughout its history.

3. Overseas Expansion: The Punic Wars, 264-201 B.C. After unifying the Italian peninsula, Rome came into conflict with Carthage, a strong city-state in North Africa. Rome was victorious in the first Punic War against Carthage and gained control of Sicily. After a difficult second war, Rome gained control of Spain and effectively ended Carthaginian power in the western Mediterranean.

4. Overseas Expansion: The Eastern Mediterranean, 200-133 B.C. In the eastern Mediterranean, Rome became involved in the affairs of the Greek city-states and Macedonia. Rome intervened on behalf of Greek allies several times before finally deciding to solve the problem by imposing direct rule in the east. Control of the Mediterranean Sea was finally completed by a last war with Carthage in which Rome annexed North Africa.

MAP EXERCISE

1.   Mark the following locations on the map: Spain, Gaul, Italy, Macedonia, Africa, Sicily, Egypt.

2.   Mark the locations of the following cities: Rome, Carthage, Alexandria, Antioch.

3.   What territory marked the region of contention between Carthage and Rome during the first Punic War? What about the geographic location of this area do you think increased the likelihood that those two cities would clash over that region?

4.   Notice the amount of Roman territory as of 265 B.C. Do you think the Romans would have fought with Carthage before that date? Why or why not?

STUDY QUESTIONS

1.   What contribution to early Roman society did the Etruscans make? How did Etruscan rule end?

2.   Describe the political structure of the early Roman society. Include military as well as social organization.

3.   How did Rome spread from a small city-state to control the Italian peninsula by 265 B.C.? What factors contributed to its military successes?

4.   Describe the Roman Republic's treatment of conquered peoples. How did this policy contribute to its success?

5.   What political system was established in the republic that allowed for sharing of power between the two classes of society? What group actually held most authority?

6.   Describe the values (including religious sensibilities) that dominated the life of the republic. How does the statue of the Roman patrician depicted in Figure 8.1 reveal these values? Which of these values did early Americans share?

7.   Describe the first two Punic Wars. What territories did Rome gain in each? Who were the generals involved? What finally happened to Carthage in the last Punic War?

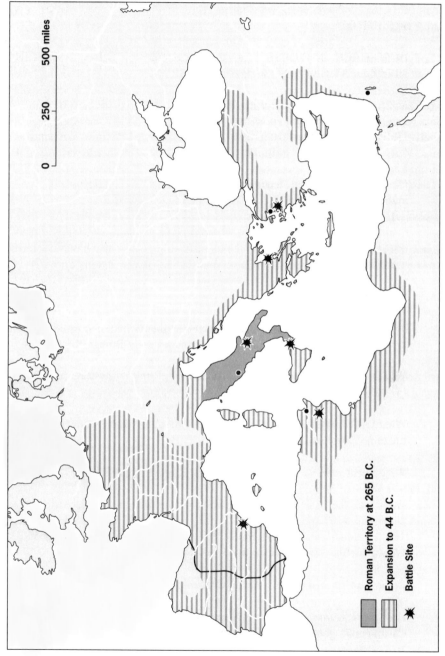

MAP 8.2 The Roman Empire, 265–44 B.C.

Roman Territory at 265 B.C.

Expansion to 44 B.C.

Battle Site

0   250   500 miles

8.   How did Rome get involved in the eastern Mediterranean? Who was its main opponent? Why did the Romans offer the Greeks such generous conditions?

IDENTIFICATION

TRY TO USE EACH OF THESE TERMS AT LEAST ONCE IN ANSWERING THE STUDY QUESTIONS AND MAP EXERCISE

*Etruscans	centuries	patricians
plebeians	legion	tribunes
*Twelve Tables	*Hannibal	*Scipio Africanus
*Punic Wars	Philip V	Macedonia
*"struggle of the orders"	consuls	clientage
	Senate	plebiscites

CHRONOLOGY

List in chronological order the words in the Identification section that have an asterisk (*). As you list these items, put a circle around those that are contemporary.

SAMPLE QUESTIONS

1.   What two peoples that originated outside the Italian peninsula brought influential advanced civilization to the resident early Romans? (p. 98)

2.   What were the two classes that made up early Rome's city-state population? (p. 100)

3.   What was the system called *clientage* that brought a force of social stability to Rome? (p. 100)

4.   What event marked the beginning of the Roman Republic? (p. 100)

5.   What was the basic military formation of the Romans that contributed to their successes? (pp. 100-101)

6.   What benefits were given to "allies" of Rome? (p. 101)

7.   Rome first clashed with Carthage over mutual interests where? (p. 104)

8.   How was Rome able to withstand and ultimately defeat the brilliant Carthaginian general, Hannibal? (p. 105)

9.   What caused Rome to change its policy in the East from one of allowing independence to one of direct Roman rule? (pp. 106-107)

10.   How did Rome annex North Africa? (p. 107)

REVIEW AND ANTICIPATION

1.   Review the Assyrian and Persian treatments of conquered peoples. Which most closely resembled the Roman model?

2.   Did Philip V of Macedon's attempts to control the Greek city-states remind you of the previous policy of Philip of Macedon and his son Alexander? Do you think the Macedonians would have been surprised at Rome's interference?

3.   Look at the map of the Roman Empire at 44 B.C. What regions do you think will be drawn into conflict with Rome next?

Chapter 9
The Failure of the Roman Republic,
133-31 B.C.

OVERVIEW

By 133 B.C., the small city-state controlled most of the Mediterranean world. The republican form of government that had grown up to satisfy the needs of the city was no longer up to the challenge of so large an empire. By 31 B.C., the republican system was in ruins, to be replaced by an imperial system of government.

1.   The Burdens of a World Power. Rome's expansion left the republic with many problems. A military system had to be established to hold the vast territories. The problems of how to govern these lands and deal equitably with the Italian allies had to be confronted. Expansion had also transformed the economic system of the peninsula. Agriculture changed from one of small holders to large estates worked by slaves. Many citizens were unemployed and lived in Rome, creating an unstable political force. Traditional values had begun to break down with exposure of new ideas. The conditions that had created the political system of the republic were no longer in place, and the republican government, controlled by a self-serving, exclusive aristocracy, had a limited ability to respond to these new problems.

2.   Attempted Reforms and Factional Struggles, 133-79 B.C. Two parties were involved in reform attempts, the *optimates* and the *populares*, and struggles between these two parties dominated this period. The Gracchi brothers attempted a series of reforms for the *populares*, that would have addressed some of the land and social problems. Powerful senators had them killed. Marius and Sulla, two strong generals who came to power on the strength of their support in the army, alternated bringing more power to the people or to the Senate. Neither succeeded in making the necessary reforms, and only demonstrated the importance of both the military and popular support in exerting power.

3.   The Era of Military Strongmen, 79-31 B.C. During a series of crises in the decade of the 70s, the Senate responded by granting extraordinary powers to strong individuals. Pompey, Crassus, and Caesar were among the first to take advantage of the situation and build their power on the military. They formed a brittle alliance that broke down in civil war among them, which Caesar won. Caesar served as dictator in Rome while preserving many of the forms of the republic. However, he was murdered by senators seeking to curb his power and return to the old forms. However, the murder simply introduced another struggle for power, which was won by Octavian. He was the sole ruler of Rome.

4.   The Fruits of Civic Strife. The century of civil strife brought devastating warfare to all Rome's territories. It also demonstrated that the republican system had become totally ineffective, and even strong dictators were unable to solve the problems that had generated such disorder. However, there were some signs that Rome would be restructured and rejuvenated. The noble class remained resilient and talented; landless plebeians formed a pool for a powerful army, and Rome had begun to take cultural leadership in the Mediterranean.

STUDY QUESTIONS

1.   What problems did Rome face in governing its newly acquired territories?

2.   How did the new wealth that Romans gained through conquest transform society? Be sure to include a discussion of agriculture and social classes.

3.   What were the reforms proposed by the Gracchi brothers? Would these have addressed the problems you analyzed in question #1? Why did they fail?

4.   Compare and contrast the careers and policies of Marius and Sulla.

5.   What were Marius' military reforms? Why were they significant for the future of Rome? Do you think they made the military too powerful a force?

6.   Who were the members of the First Triumvirate? Upon what did each base his power? Why did the alliance break down? Who won sole leadership?

7.   Discuss the importance of the military in all the political events between 79-31 B.C. How did each of the strongmen come to power? Could they have done so without the support of an army?

8.   What reforms did Julius Caesar attempt? Would his reforms have addressed the problems that the Gracchi brothers addressed? Why was Caesar murdered?

9.   Who were the members of the Second Triumvirate? Why did the alliance break down? Who won sole leadership?

10.   What were some positive signs of Roman strength by 31 B.C. that heralded the possibility for Rome's recovery from the devastation of the century?

IDENTIFICATION

TRY TO USE EACH OF THESE TERMS AT LEAST ONCE IN ANSWERING
THE STUDY QUESTIONS

latifundia	*equites*	proletariat
Epicureanism	Stoicism	*Tiberius Gracchus
*Gaius Gracchus	*Marius	*Sulla
*Social War	*Pompey	*Crassus
*Julius Caesar	Cicero	*Mark Antony
*Octavian	Cleopatra	*optimates*
populares	*Spartacus	

CHRONOLOGY

List in chronological order the words in the Identification section that have an asterisk
(*). As you list these items, put a circle around those that are contemporary.

SAMPLE QUESTIONS

1.   Contrast Rome's policies toward its Italian allies with those of non-Italian
       territories. (p. 110)

2.   Who were the *equites* and why were they important? (p. 111)

3.   Who were the proletariat, and why were they important? (p. 111)

4.   What new ideas began to transform traditional Roman values? (p. 111)

5.   What was the real political issue that made Tiberius Gracchus so threatening
       to the Senate? (p. 112)

6.   What were three of the policies advocated by Gaius Gracchus? (p. 113)

7.   What reforms did Marius make in the military? (p. 113)

8.   What were the issues in the Social War? (p. 113)

9.   What reforms did Pompey make to solidify provincial administration? (p.
       115)

10.   What office did Julius Caesar hold, and on what was his real power based?
       (p. 117)

11.   Who supported Cleopatra in her struggle for power against her brother/husband? (p. 116)

12.   What happened to Cleopatra and her empire with the victory of Octavian? (p. 118)

13.   What efforts were made during the late republic to resolve Rome's urban problems? (p. 120)

REVIEW AND ANTICIPATION

1.   Review the Hellenistic philosophies of Epicureanism and Stoicism. How was the situation of the late Roman Republic similar to that of the large Hellenistic states that spawned these philosophies?

2.   Review the establishment of the Hellenistic kingdom of the Ptolemies. What strengths did that kingdom have that made it desirable for Rome to annex?

3.   What kind of government will Rome establish with the fall of the republican form? What do you think will be the strengths and what will be the weaknesses of any new government?

Chapter 10
The Roman Empire and the *Pax Romana*,
31 B.C.-A.D. 180

OVERVIEW

After the fall of the Roman Republic, the Romans created a political order, the empire, that endured, brought a measure of peace to the Mediterranean world, and spread Greco-Roman culture over a vast area.

1.   Octavian's New Political Order, 31 B.C.-A.D. 14. Octavian wisely established a government that attempted to preserve the traditions of Rome, yet offered the stability of a strong rule. He accepted a wide range of titles and privileges that endowed him with so much authority that he virtually ruled single-handedly. He clarified the roles of all the classes and established a bureaucracy that worked efficiently. He stabilized the army and kept it under his control. Finally, he established a form of succession that was to ensure continuity of his system.

2.   Testing the Augustan Establishment, A.D. 14-96. Although Augustus intended to establish a smooth succession, it was not fully successful. Many of the subsequent emperors were violent and corrupt, and succession was seldom smooth. In spite of these problems, the system he had set up to run the empire functioned effectively, and by the end of the century it was popularly believed that rule by a *princeps* was the only guarantee of peace and prosperity.

3.   *Pax Romana*: The "Good Emperors," A.D. 96-180. The "Roman Peace" was introduced with the reign of Trajan, and continued through the next four emperors. These men consolidated Rome's expansion at the frontiers, and introduced measures that brought increased peace and prosperity to the empire.

4.   The Nature of the Imperial Political Order. In theory, the imperial order was a highly structured system in which power was vested in the emperor and exercised through a bureaucracy. This hierarchy was supplemented by local city-state governments. In reality, the highly personal nature of the imperial order led to household servants and private contractors exerting considerable power. The breakdown in the clear hierarchy led to local city-state governments becoming increasingly important. The system worked because the nobility (from Rome to the provinces) preserved a strong sense of duty and service that usually led to good government regardless of structural inadequacies.

5.   <u>Economic and Social Life in the Roman Empire.</u> In general, the prosperity increased during the empire, although it was never evenly distributed. Agriculture remained the basis of the economy, but rural laborers fell increasingly into dependency. Trade and industry expanded, particularly fueled by the building boom that characterized imperial policy. Roman citizenry remained carefully divided into classes: nobles, *equites*, plebeians, and slaves. Women gained considerable control over their lives and property. Plebeians and slaves seldom shared in the prosperity of the empire.

MAP EXERCISE

See map on p. 46.

1.   Which of the shaded areas represents Roman expansion during the republic, and which expansion through the third century? Of the areas acquired in the third century, which do you think were wealthy enough to have provided income for Rome, and which might have been a drain on economic resources?

2.   Which of the shaded areas represents territory temporarily controlled? Why was that region particularly vulnerable and difficult for Rome to hold?

3.   During the late empire, Rome had an increasingly difficult time with frontier defense. Looking at the extent of the empire on the map, that makes sense. What regions will be particularly vulnerable to attack? What kinds of natural geographical features did Rome treat as boundaries to help in defense?

4.   Where is Hadrian's wall? Why was it built?

STUDY QUESTIONS

1.   How did Octavian (Augustus) manage to take full power while seeming to preserve the traditions of Rome? Was it clear which of the powers belonged to the *princeps* and which to the Senate and people? How did this appear as a problem?

2.   In the imperial system of government, what were the responsibilities of the three free classes of the empire (*nobiles, equites,* and plebeians)? Describe the way of life of each of these groups. What was the situation of the peasants and slaves?

3.   What reforms did Augustus make in the army? How were these reforms intended to keep the army from becoming the destabilizing force it had been during the years of civil war? Did they work?

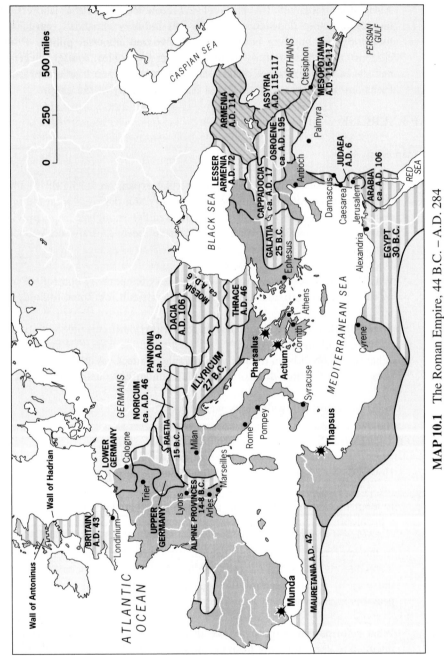

MAP 10.1 The Roman Empire, 44 B.C. – A.D. 284

4.   What mechanism for ensuring a smooth succes
        What was wrong with this method as it w
        Claudians? What solution to the succession pro
        the era of the "good emperors" (96-180 A.D.)?

5.   What kinds of reforms were introduced by the
        A.D.) that helped secure internal peace in the en
        commonwealth guided from Rome?

6.   In what ways did the imperial system encourage economic prosperity? Who
        benefited most by this growth? Who benefited least?

7.   Although the economy of the empire remained agriculturally based, city life
        was seen as central to Roman life. What were the benefits and drawbacks of
        city life? Were they the same for the rich and the poor?

IDENTIFICATION

TRY TO USE EACH OF THESE TERMS AT LEAST ONCE IN ANSWERING
THE STUDY QUESTIONS

*Octavian	*princeps*	Praetorian Guard
*Tiberius	*Julio-Claudians	*Flavians
*Marcus Aurelius	*legatus*	*procurator*
nobiles	*equites*	*imperator*
*Claudius	*Nero	*Vespasian
*Trajan	*Hadrian	

CHRONOLOGY

List in chronological order the words in the Identification section that have an asterisk
(*). As you list these items, put a circle around those that are contemporary.

SAMPLE QUESTIONS

1.   What steps did Octavian take to revive a feeling of pride in Rome? (p. 124)

2.   Why was the Praetorian Guard created? (p. 124)

3.   What was the key element of Octavian's fiscal system that was to ensure
        enough money to support his new governmental order? (p. 125)

4.   What was the main weakness in the Augustan system that presented a
        constant source of tension? (p. 126)

What was the main international problem faced by the "good emperors," Hadrian and Marcus Aurelius? (p. 127)

6. What legal reforms did the "good emperors" make for the empire? (p. 128)

7. What officials represented the emperor's authority in the provinces, and what were their responsibilities? (p. 128)

8. How did personal imperial household servants end up becoming the real power wielders of the empire? (p. 129)

9. More than anything else, what was it that caused the Roman world to be guided in a common direction that prized peace and order? (p. 129)

10. What regions of the empire produced large surpluses of grain for export? (p. 130)

11. What kinds of governmental involvement introduced an element of instability into the economic system? (p. 131)

12. What rights did Roman women have before the law? (pp. 131-32)

REVIEW AND ANTICIPATION

1. Review the reasons for Julius Caesar's murder. How did Octavian avoid the same fate?

2. Review Stoicism. In what ways were Marcus Aurelius' policies consistent with the principles of Stoicism? In general, do you think Stoics would make good rulers?

3. Contrast the position of women in the Greek city-states with their position in the Roman Empire. Which is closer to our modern life?

4. What do you think will be the cause of the fall of this empire?

Chapter 11
Roman Thought and Expression

OVERVIEW

Romans not only conquered the Mediterranean world with armies and political structures, but they also disseminated Greek culture that they modified with their own distinctive style. Their cultural productions decisively influenced the future in western Europe.

1. Rome and the Reception of Greek Culture. Traditional Romans had little interest in cultural pursuits. This changed when their expansion brought them into contact with Hellenistic culture. They reorganized their educational system to incorporate Hellenistic thought, and adopted Hellenistic architectural and artistic styles. Even the masses were Hellenized, particularly by the increased popularity of mystery religions.

2. Roman Literature. Roman literature was profoundly important in the history of western culture. Roman poets expressed the glory of Rome and the passions and moral power of individuals. Prose writers expressed political positions and wrote eloquent histories. Greek literature continued to flourish under the tolerant cultural environment of Roman rule.

3. Roman Art. The Romans borrowed extensively from the Greeks. Their most impressive achievements were in architecture, where they developed new techniques and used them most impressively in large public buildings. The sculptors were by and large less innovative, copying Greek works. However, they did excel in portrait sculptures. Painters extensively decorated the buildings.

4. Roman Philosophy, Science, and Religion. Roman philosophers applied Hellenistic philosophy to their own particular culture. Some advocated Epicurean ideals of withdrawal from the world, but more popular was Stoicism, modified to give greater attention to social responsibility. Neoplatonism stressed the superiority of the spiritual world and advocated mystical experiences. Romans were less interested in science than in practical applications of technology. Their scientific advances tended to be limited to compiling encyclopedias of existing knowledge. Roman religion emphasized public ritual, leading to emperor-worship, but at the same time there was a growth of personal mystery religions.

5. Roman Law. One of the most influential creations of Rome was its law. Throughout their history, Romans focused on the law as a guarantor of citizens' rights. A rich body of law developed that included law of citizens.

Along with this, decisions of judges and their advisers became established as precedents. Further laws were created for noncitizens, and finally the concept of "natural law" was developed that stood above all else and served as an organizing principle.

6.   The Romans and Cultural Diffusion. The Romans spread their culture all over the empire, but the impact was greatest in the West, which had not previously been exposed to Hellenization. There were many ways by which the culture was spread, and it served to bring many people under the sway of a common culture that would influence their histories for centuries.

STUDY QUESTIONS

1.   Describe the changes in education that came about with the "discovery" of Greek culture by the Romans. What subjects were stressed? To what degree did young women participate in the new education?

2.   What themes did the Romans favor in their literature? How were these themes consistent with their interests in good government and moral virtue? Discuss the works of three writers that demonstrate these interests.

3.   What did the poetry of Vergil and the history of Livy have in common?

4.   Describe Rome's achievements in the field of architecture. What were their innovations, and how were they used in some of the best examples of Roman architecture? On what kinds of buildings did the Romans expend most of their talents and much of their money?

5.   Discuss the Romans' adaptation of Hellenistic philosophy. Who were the main philosophers? What elements of these philosophies were particularly suited to Roman temperament?

6.   Who compiled the Roman encyclopedias that preserved scientific knowledge in geography, natural history, astronomy and medicine? What kind of science did the Romans favor over pure science?

7.   What were the three kinds of laws developed during the empire? Which do you think ultimately will be the most influential?

8.   What was the process by which Roman culture was spread throughout the empire? What do you think was the most important element in this diffusion?

IDENTIFICATION

TRY TO USE EACH OF THESE TERMS AT LEAST ONCE IN ANSWERING THE STUDY QUESTIONS

Dionysus	Isis	Vergil
Aeneid	Catullus	Horace
Lucretius	Cicero	Livy
Tacitus	Suetonius	colosseum
Pantheon	forum	basilica
Plotinus	Neoplatonism	Strabo
Pliny the Elder	Ptolemy	Galen
ius civile	*ius gentium*	natural law
Marcus Aurelius	Seneca	Cato the Elder

SAMPLE QUESTIONS

1. What two courses of study became the touchstone for the new education? (p. 136)

2. In what way were the masses of people most touched by Hellenization? (p. 136)

3. Who wrote the *Aeneid*, and what was its main theme? (p. 137)

4. What themes that reflect the character of the Romans were emphasized by poets like Lucretius and Horace? (pp. 137-138)

5. Instead of fiction, what kinds of literature did the Romans favor? (p. 138)

6. The prose writings of whom set a model for Latin prose that would be imitated for centuries and continues to be studied today? (p. 138)

7. Give three architectural innovations of the Romans. (p. 139)

8. What did the best Roman sculpture depict? (p. 140)

9. From the few examples of Roman painting that remain, what were the favorite themes of painters? (p. 141)

10. What emperor was known for his Stoic writings, and what did he emphasize in his particular style of Stoicism? (p. 142)

11. What are the main elements of Neoplatonism? (p. 142)

12.   What did the Romans mean by "natural law?" (pp. 143-144)

13.   What modern languages are direct descendants of Latin? (p. 144)

REVIEW AND ANTICIPATION

1.   Review classical Greek cultural accomplishments. In what ways did the Romans depart most from their Greek predecessors? Why?

2.   Review the cultural achievements of the Hellenistic states. In what ways were the Roman cultural achievements similar to those of the Hellenistic states?

3.   Which of the cultural accomplishments discussed in this chapter do you think will have the most impact in the short term (next few centuries) and the long term (until now)?

Chapter 12
Crisis in the Roman World, A.D. 180-284:
Conflict, Change, and Christianity

OVERVIEW

In the third century, the Roman Empire that seemed so enduring experienced a series of political, economic, social, and cultural crises that would deeply test the structure of the empire. Furthermore, a new force appeared, Christianity, that would ultimately radically transform the empire.

1.   Constitutional Problems. Weaknesses inherent in the *principate* established by Augustus became extremely apparent in the third century. The problem of the succession came forward again as emperors attempted to leave the office to incapable sons. The army became emperor-makers again, leading to civil wars. The defense of the frontiers became a large problem as more incursions into the borders were made. This problem increased the power of the army. These pressures led to a change in the nature of the office of emperor, who was no longer "first citizen," but rather absolute lord.

2.   Economic, Social, and Cultural Stresses. The empire in the third century experienced economic depression, caused by a decline in agricultural production, falling population, and a debased coinage leading to inflation. The old social structure, too, began to change. The old aristocracy was no longer as important a factor in a political balance that increasingly centered on the military. The new privileged groups were great landholders and soldiers. In these turbulent times, people increasingly turned to religion.

3.   Christianity: Origins. Christianity began in a Judaic environment that was torn by competing ideas on how best to live and practice their religion under the rule of Rome. Jesus was born into this turmoil, and he preached a message of spiritual redemption to Jews, neglecting no one, even the poor and women. He was crucified by the Romans as part of their effort to suppress discontent in the province.

4.   The Spread of Christianity. Followers of Jesus, the apostles, carried Christian ideas to many cities. Saul of Tarsus (Paul) was influential in preaching to non-Jews and making Christianity have wider appeal than simply as a Jewish sect. Christianity separated more from Judaism and gained many converts. By the end of the third century, in spite of periodic persecution, Christian communities were well established in the cities of the empire.

5.   <u>The Transformation of Early Christianity.</u> As Christianity spread throughout the empire, it underwent some transformations. Christian thought was influenced by Greco-Roman thought and language, and philosophy. Elaborate ritual practices were adopted that included complex ceremonies to mark important times of life. Finally, a complex, hierarchic organization was developed that included bishops and priests, and slowly the Bishop of Rome began to assume preeminence over this hierarchy.

6.   <u>Christianity and the Crisis in the Roman World.</u> While Christians operated within the Roman world, many certainly must have focused their attention on the next world. Their rituals and organization created a community that made them separate. The growth of Christianity was one more force that caused the empire to be transformed.

MAP EXERCISE

1.   Locate the following cities: Jerusalem, Alexandria, Antioch, Constantinople, Carthage, Rome.

2.   In what part of the empire was Christianity strongest by the beginning of the fourth century? Why? Do you think this is going to lead to an increased Hellenization of Christian beliefs?

3.   Do most of the Christian centers seem to coincide with regions of commerce? Why do you think that would be so?

STUDY QUESTIONS

1.   What were the constitutional problems faced in the third century? How did these problems tend to increase the power of the army?

2.   How did the increased militarization of the political world contribute to economic problems in the empire?

3.   What social changes accompanied the third-century crises? What groups lost political power and what groups gained?

4.   What were four different "sects" in Judaism that represented differing ways to address living under the control of Rome? After the destruction of the Temple, which group became predominant?

5.   Where do we get the evidence for the historical Jesus? What are the main problems in using these sources? What seems to be the main message of Jesus that emerged from these texts?

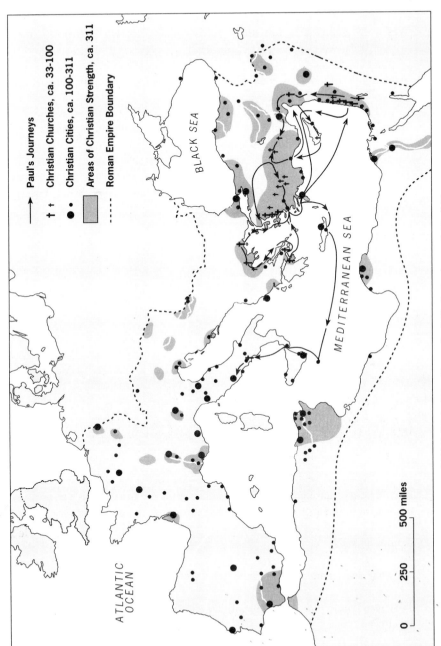

Paul's Journeys

- → Paul's Journeys
- † † Christian Churches, ca. 33–100
- • • Christian Cities, ca. 100–311
- ▨ Areas of Christian Strength, ca. 311
- ----- Roman Empire Boundary

ATLANTIC OCEAN

BLACK SEA

MEDITERRANEAN SEA

0   250   500 miles

MAP 12.1   The Spread of Christianity to A.D. 311

6.   Describe the process by which Christians increasingly separated themselves from Jews. Who and what events facilitated and increased this separation?

7.   Why were some early Christians persecuted by Romans? What was their crime? What were the rumors about them?

8.   What kinds of changes took place in Christianity as it was increasingly exposed to Greco-Roman thought?

9.   What kinds of rituals dominated religious practice during the Apostolic Age? What kinds were added as the Church spread?

10.   Describe the growing organization of the Church. How was the hierarchy structured? On what basis did bishops claim authority? What bishops emerged as most powerful?

IDENTIFICATION

TRY TO USE EACH OF THESE TERMS AT LEAST ONCE IN ANSWERING THE STUDY QUESTIONS AND MAP EXERCISES

*Septimius Severus	*Tiberius	*Jesus
Sadducees	Pharisees	Zealots
Essenes	Diaspora	*Pontius Pilate
*"barracks	*Paul	Apostolic Age
emperors"	*Origen	bishop
*Clement	Petrine theory	pope
apostolic	*Dead Sea Scrolls	*Peter
succession		

CHRONOLOGY

List in chronological order the words in the Identification section that have an asterisk (*). As you list these items, put a circle around those that are contemporary.

SAMPLE QUESTIONS

1.   To what does the term "barracks emperors" refer? (p. 147)

2.   Why was the defense of the frontier an increasing issue in the third century? (p. 147)

3.   What effect did the emergence of autocratic imperial leadership have on local government? (p. 148)

4.   What economic policy that led to inflation did the emperors pursue in their search for funds to reward the army? (p. 148)

5.   Why did the imperial government give increasing freedom to great landowners? (p. 149)

6.   How did the Zealots react to Roman rule of the Jewish homeland? (p. 151)

7.   What are the earliest surviving documents about the teachings of Jesus, and how long after Jesus' death were they written? (p. 152)

8.   During the reign of which emperor was Jesus probably crucified? (p. 153)

9.   What were the ways the first generation of Christians prepared themselves for the second coming of Christ? (p. 153)

10.   Under what emperor was Paul martyred? (p. 154)

11.   How did the authors of the New Testament interpret the Jewish Bible? (p. 156)

12.   What is the theory of "apostolic succession," and what did it provide for? (p. 158)

13.   Explain the "Petrine theory." (p. 158)

REVIEW AND ANTICIPATION

1.   Review the treatment of peasants and landworkers in general during the late republic and early principate. In what ways did this early neglect contribute to the third-century crisis?

2.   Review the characteristics of the ancient Hebrews that had set them apart from the world of the ancient Middle East. How many of those characteristics were shared by the early Christians? In what ways were the early Christians different?

3.   With all the crises that confronted the Roman Empire in the third century, is it likely that the empire would continue to stand? Which of these problems do you think will ultimately bring down the empire?

Chapter 13
Late Antiquity, A.D. 284-500:
The End of Greco-Roman Civilization

OVERVIEW

The crisis of the third century generated reforms that preserved the empire through the fourth century. However, the pressure of the Germanic invaders broke up the old political unity and established new kingdoms in western Europe.

1.   The Reforms of Diocletian and Constantine. Emperor Diocletian instituted reforms to address the third-century crises: He restructured the empire politically and divided the rule; he increased the army and made it more mobile; he froze occupations, prices and wages, and in general imposed an authoritarian regime. His successor, Constantine, continued many of his policies, but abandoned Diocletian's persecution of Christians in favor of tolerance supported by imperial patronage.

2.   An Uneasy Peace. While the reforms helped for a while, there were fundamental problems in the empire that were not addressed. There were increased disparities of wealth between individuals and regions of the empire; the costly autocratic regime caused many people, rich and poor alike, to avoid civic responsibility, and even Christians were divided over doctrinal issues.

3.   The Germans. The Germans were organized into tribes that emphasized warfare and kinship ties. They had distinctive legal traditions based on compensation for injuries. They were polytheistic with a highly developed oral tradition and artistic talent for metal work. By the fourth century, these tribes were beginning to organize into larger groups with a more complex military structure. They had interacted enough with the empire to be aware of its material wealth.

4.   The Germanic Migrations: The Disruption of the Roman Empire. By the fifth century, Roman defenses were no longer adequate for keeping out the Germanic peoples. Many invaded the empire and settled in the western portion, establishing virtually independent kingdoms. The empire in the East remained intact. Germanic rule did not cause complete disruption of the old ways of life. Instead, the economic decentralization that had begun as early as the third century continued.

5.   Christianity in Late Antiquity. The success of the spread of Christianity was demonstrated when Theodosius proclaimed Christianity the state religion. However, this success led to transformations in the Church to change it from

a movement distrustful of authority to a corporate ent'
members. One change included increasing the hierar'
Church and the sanctions against disobedience. So'
this more worldly church by withdrawing to see'
hermits or in monasteries. Others worked withh.
increasing the intermingling of secular and religious a...
concern with doctrinal uniformity led to some people being identn...
"heretics" who disagreed with doctrine and were persecuted by Christians for
their beliefs. Some Christians became actively involved in artistic and
intellectual pursuits, creating beautiful churches and powerful writings that
shaped the future of western thought.

MAP EXERCISE

See map on p. 60.

1. Write on the map the areas where the following peoples settled: Vandals,
    Franks, Visigoths, Ostrogoths, Lombards, Angles, Saxons, Jutes, Celts.

2. Which area of the Roman Empire remained free of large settlements of
    Germanic peoples? Does this pattern indicate in what way the empire will be
    divided?

3. Where is Constantinople? Why is this site strategically important?

STUDY QUESTIONS

1. Describe the political restructuring of the empire introduced by Diocletian.
    Include how the role of emperor changed, and what new hierarchy was
    developed to facilitate his rule.

2. What were Diocletian's economic reforms? Do you think they addressed the
    underlying economic problems discussed in the previous chapter? What
    economic problems continued and even got worse after Constantine's reign?

3. In what ways did Constantine support and encourage the growth of
    Christianity in the empire?

4. How did some people escape from civic responsibility during the late
    empire? How disruptive do you think such actions will be?

5. Describe the political and social organization of the Germans. How was the
    king chosen? What was the role of women? By the fourth century, what
    changes were taking place in their traditional society?

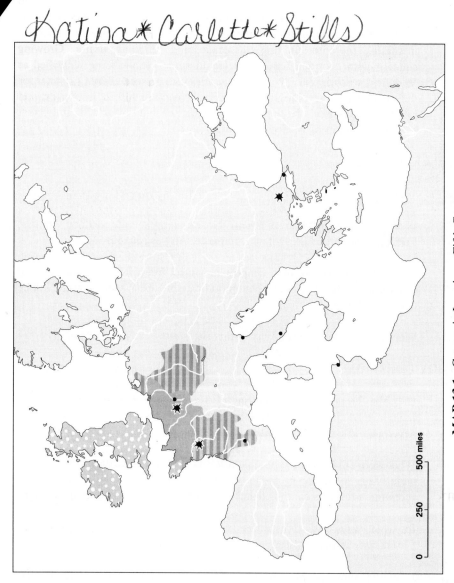

MAP 13.1 Germanic Invasions, Fifth Century

0   250   500 miles

6. Describe the legal system of the Germans. Which of the provisions seem most strange to us?

7. In what ways did the Germanic settlements in the West change the old empire and in what ways did they not? Why did many Romans not bother to fight to expel the invaders?

8. What changes did Christianity undergo after it became the official church of the empire? Who objected to these changes? Do you think some people will continue to object?

9. Describe the two kinds of monastic life. Why do you think these holy people will continue to be influential?

10. What were the main ideas of the three western Church Fathers, Ambrose, Jerome, and Augustine? How did they transform the old Greco-Roman ideals?

IDENTIFICATION

TRY TO USE EACH OF THESE TERMS AT LEAST ONCE IN ANSWERING THE STUDY QUESTIONS AND MAP EXERCISES

*Diocletian	*Constantine	*Edict of Milan
praetorian prefect	*Helen	dioceses
*Theodosius	*Julian	*wergeld*
compurgation	ordeal	*comitatus*
*Alaric	*Clovis	*Theoderic
Attila	*Odoacer	Anthony
*Ambrose	*Augustine	*Jerome
Donatism	Arianism	Nicene Creed
Church Fathers	Vulgate	*Leo I

CHRONOLOGY

List in chronological order the words in the Identification section that have an asterisk (*). As you list these items, put a circle around those that are contemporary.

SAMPLE QUESTIONS

1. What policy for an orderly succession did Diocletian introduce? (p. 162)

2. What policy of Diocletian reduced the traditionally active local city-state governments? (p. 162)

3.   What was the Edict of Milan? (p. 163)

4.   To where did Constantine move the capital of the empire? (p. 164)

5.   How would peasants escape taxation and other burdens imposed on them by the empire? (p. 165)

6.   What was Emperor Julian's religious policy? (p. 165)

7.   What was Emperor Theodosius' religious policy? (p. 165)

8.   Where was the original homeland of the Germans? (p. 166)

9.   What was the principal preoccupation of German law? (p. 166)

10.   What was the significance of the newly developing institution of war bands (*comitatus*) among the Germans? (p. 167)

11.   Who deposed the last Roman emperor in the West? (p. 169)

12.   What was the main theme of the *City of God*? (p. 176)

13.   What was the significance of the Vulgate Bible? (p. 177)

REVIEW AND ANTICIPATION

1.   Review the strengths and virtues that had made the early Roman Republic so successful. How many of those were lost by the fourth-century reforms of Diocletian and Constantine? Do you think that loss contributed to the decline of the empire?

2.   Review the Roman legal principles. In what ways do you think the German legal system departs most strikingly from the Roman? Do you think it will be difficult to reconcile the two?

3.   Review the map in Chapter 12 of the spread of Christianity. Locate Carthage. What famous Church Father was located near there? Does this map help explain why that region became such a center for Christian thought in the fourth and fifth centuries?

4.   Look at the map in this chapter. Which of these Germanic tribes are located in a position that makes it more likely that they could create an empire in Europe?

Chapter 14
Heirs to the Roman Empire:
The Byzantine and Moslem Empires

OVERVIEW

The Mediterranean unity of the old Roman Empire broke up into three distinct culture units: The western kingdoms, the Byzantine Empire, and the Moslem Empire. The latter two were highly sophisticated, prosperous civilizations.

1. Byzantine Civilization: Origins and History, 395-1100. The Byzantine Empire was the heir to the old Roman Empire in the East. Justinian attempted to reconquer the western portions, but that attempt was wasteful and unsuccessful. After Justinian, the Byzantine Empire was constantly confronting threats from the north and from the east. Strong emperors held off attacks, but the Byzantine Empire was reduced in territory.

2. Byzantine Civilization: Institutional and Cultural Patterns. The Byzantine Empire had a tightly organized administration that was based on absolute authority of the emperor controlling both state and church. The army was well organized and well funded by a prosperous commercial and agricultural economy. The Eastern Church, centered at Constantinople, was increasingly differentiated from the West, separated by language, questions of who should rule, and dogma. Finally, the two churches separated in 1054, leaving the "Greek Orthodox Church" dominant in the East. Byzantine culture stressed learning, ensured the preservation of Greek learning, and developed sophisticated and beautiful architecture and art.

3. Islamic Civilization: Origins and Early History. Muhammad, a prophet born in Mecca, proclaimed a new religion that spread rapidly from the Arabian Desert throughout the Near East and the southern Mediterranean to India. The religion spread rapidly in part by the striking military conquests of the Arabs. The religion, called Islam, was based on the holy book, the Koran, and required its followers to submit to the authority of a monotheistic God. Believers were also supposed to pray, attend mosque, fast through one month, and make a pilgrimage to Mecca.

4. Islamic Civilization: Institutional and Cultural Patterns. Political leadership of the Moslem world was taken by a *caliph* who interpreted and applied the laws defined by the Koran. Political unity broke down as various dynasties of caliphs emerged and conflicting opinions arose over who was to rule. The Moslem world prospered because of extensive commerce. As the religion grew more complicated, differences of opinion created several branches of Islam. Moslem thinkers made significant contributions to science and

philosophy, and architects created magnificent houses of worship, beautifully decorated in geometric patterns.

MAP EXERCISE

1.   Indicate on the map the following political entities: Visigothic Kingdom, Kingdom of the Franks, Kingdom of the Lombards, Byzantine Empire, Moslem Empire.

2.   Where are the following cities: Mecca, Medina, Damascus, Constantinople, Alexandria, Jerusalem, Baghdad, Toledo, Tours?

3.   What city was the capital of the Omayyad dynasty? What was the capital of the Abbasid dynasty? What was the significance of the change?

4.   Locate the origin of the Moslem world. Where was Muhammad born?

5.   Which of the western kingdoms will be on the front line of defense against Islam? Where will the Byzantine Empire have to fortify most strongly?

STUDY QUESTIONS

1.   What were Justinian's main and most enduring accomplishments? What was his most obvious failure? Which of his accomplishments do you think will have the longest-term impact?

2.   Describe the struggle of the Byzantine emperors after Justinian to withstand invasions. Which of its neighbors do you think will pose the greatest threat?

3.   How was the Byzantine Empire organized? What were its strengths (include political, military, and economic strengths)?

4.   How was the religious life and development in the Byzantine Empire different from that of the West? Do you think it was inevitable that the two churches would split? Why or why not?

5.   In what artistic fields did the Byzantines excel? Why?

6.   What were the beliefs and practices of Islam? In what ways was it similar to Christianity and Judaism, and in what ways did it differ?

7.   What factors contributed to Islam's rapid and successful spread?

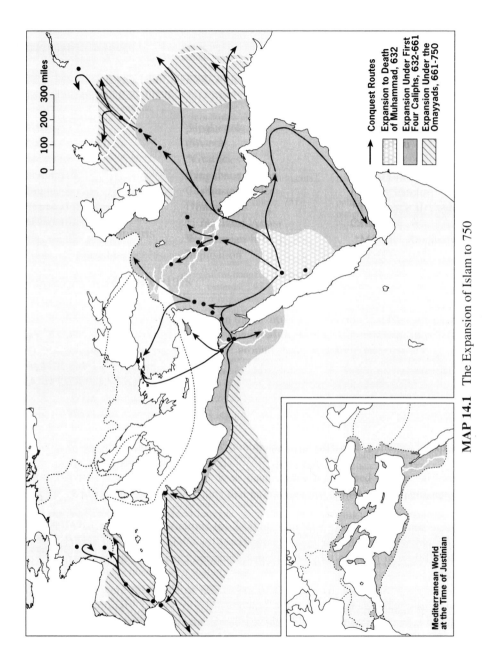

MAP 14.1 The Expansion of Islam to 750

8.   What was the political organization of the Islamic world? What divisive forces appeared in the Moslem world? How did the first two dynasties exemplify one of the divisive forces?

9.   Describe the economic life of the Moslem world. What things stimulated their advanced commercial development?

10.   What were the philosophic and scientific advances developed in the Moslem world? Which will be most influential in the long term?

IDENTIFICATION

TRY TO USE EACH OF THESE TERMS AT LEAST ONCE IN ANSWERING THE STUDY QUESTIONS AND MAP EXERCISES

*Justinian	*Theodora	*Corpus juris
Santa Sophia	*Heraclius	civilis*
caesaropapism	*Leo III	iconoclasm
Procopius	Anna Comnenus	*Muhammad
Koran	*Kaaba*	Islam
Moslem	*Hegira*	mosque
*Charles Martel	caliph	Ali
*Omayyads	Shiites	*Abbasid
Sunnite	*sufis*	Avicenna
Averroës	Lombards	Seljuk Turks
Bedouins	*Basil II	

CHRONOLOGY

List in chronological order the words in the Identification section that have an asterisk (*). As you list these items, put a circle around those that are contemporary.

SAMPLE QUESTIONS

1.   What was the result of Justinian's attempt to reunify the empire? (p. 183)

2.   Why was the *Corpus juris civilis* so important? (pp. 183-184)

3.   How did the Byzantine emperor manage to keep the loyalty of peasant soldiers? (p. 186)

4.   How is the term "caesaropapism" appropriate to the Byzantine emperor? (p. 187)

5. What was the "iconoclastic controversy" about? (p. 187)

6. What did the Byzantine visual artists try to accomplish and evoke in their work? (p. 189)

7. What was the main long-term significance of the Byzantines' conversion of the Slavs? (pp. 187-188)

8. What year marks the first year of the Moslem calendar, and what happened in that year? (p. 190)

9. What did Muhammad believe was Jesus' role in history? (p. 190)

10. What battle stopped the Moslem advance in the West? (p. 191)

11. What distinguishes Shiite Moslems from Sunnis? (p. 194)

12. Why did all Moslems have to learn Arabic? (p. 195)

13. Why did Moslems use floral and geometric patterns in their artwork? (p. 196)

REVIEW AND ANTICIPATION

1. How did the Persians successfully govern their large empire? What elements of their rule were adopted by the Moslems?

2. Review the reforms of Diocletian and Constantine. Which of their policies were continued by the Byzantine rulers? Why were they more enduring in the East than they had been in the western portions of the empire?

Chapter 15
Heirs to the Roman Empire:
Latin Western Europe

OVERVIEW

As the western portion of the old Roman Empire disintegrated, it exhibited much less stability than the other two cultural areas. Several centuries would pass before new institutions and ideas emerged from the decentralization that accompanied the fall of the empire in the West.

1.   The Political Order: Germanic Kingship. Between 500 and 750 A.D., the western kingdoms were dominated by two factors which led to a good deal of instability: 1) the lack of fixed boundaries between the kingdoms, and 2) the lack of centralized political structures. By 750, warfare among the kingdoms had roughly determined settled borders, but the problem of central authority was more difficult. This chapter looks at the example of the Franks. The Frankish dynasty attempted to establish a strong kingship on the Roman model without the skills to do so. Consequently, landed nobles acquired more power and reduced the central authority.

2.   Economic and Social Patterns. Economic production in the West sank to low levels. Agriculture was conducted on large villas by tenants, in village communities, or on individual farms. As the social structure changed, a new landed aristocracy emerged, who dominated semifree peasants. This aristocracy focused on tight family ties, violence and feuds. Women held an important social position.

3.   Religious Life. Religious life in the West at the beginning of the sixth century suffered from increased disunity, worldly leaders, and weakened religious consciousness. Two institutions, the papacy and monasticism, led in the restoration of religious structures. Popes like Gregory I were involved in theological, social and pastoral efforts that served to strengthen the role of the papacy in church leadership. Benedict of Nursia established a rule for monks that stressed obedience to authority and made monasticism a powerful force for enhanced religious life.

4.   Cultural Life. During this period, much of the cultural life focused on preserving the classical and patristic literature of the past. Some courts served as patrons, but most of the learning was preserved in monasteries, where churchmen and women preserved the Latin of the ancient texts. Some of the Germanic oral works were written down, and Germanic designs influenced the art of the time.

STUDY QUESTIONS

1. What was the political structure established by the Merovingians? Why were the kings unable to exercise the power they claimed? Who became more powerful as a result of this failure?

2. What mechanisms did the landed nobility use to increase their power?

3. Historians divide time into convenient blocks at seemingly significant turning points. What three periods are suggested as the turning points for the end of the Greco-Roman world? What is the argument in favor of each? Which does your text seem to support by its organization?

4. How was agricultural production organized in the early medieval West?

5. What social structure had emerged in the West? Describe the social classes. What was their life like? What was the position of women?

6. In what ways had the religious institutions and sensibilities been weakened in the West by the fall of the Roman Empire?

7. What ways did the Church in the West develop to counteract these forces and strengthen the Church again? What institutions were most important in this effort? How?

8. What role did monasteries play in sustaining society's cultural life after the fifth century?

9. What works written between the fifth and the eighth centuries were central in the preservation of classical learning?

10. Discuss how the visual arts combined Germanic and Celtic artistic forms with Christian and classical styles. Refer to the *Book of Kells* (Color Plate 8) to illustrate your discussion.

IDENTIFICATION

TRY TO USE EACH OF THESE TERMS AT LEAST ONCE IN ANSWERING THE STUDY QUESTIONS

Merovingian	*Bede	*Patrick
vassals	counts	*Benedict of Nursia
*Gregory I	*Leo I	*Isidore of Seville
*Boethius	*Clovis	*Beowulf*

potentes	*Gregory of Tours	*Book of Kells*
*Gelasius I	commendation	Benedictine Rule
pauperes		

CHRONOLOGY

List in chronological order the words in the Identification section that have an asterisk (*). As you list these items, put a circle around those that are contemporary.

SAMPLE QUESTIONS

1.   How did King Clovis' conversion to orthodox Christianity help strengthen his rule? (p. 198) •

2.   What did Merovingian kings do with the inheritance of their kingdom? (p. 200)

3.   Why were people willing to enroll as dependents to a powerful person? (pp. 200-201)

4.   Who conducted what little long-distance trade remained in the West? (p. 201)

5.   What was the most important technological advance of this period that allowed agricultural exploitation of land north of the Alps? (p. 202)

6.   What kinds of activities did the Church begin to take on that fulfilled an important social role in communities? (p. 203)

7.   What was Pope Gelasius I's position on the relationship between church and state? (p. 204)

8.   What was the key feature of Benedictine communities that helped make them such an important force for unity in the Church? (p. 206)

9.   Describe the work of Bede and tell why it is so important. (pp. 206-207)

10.   Give one example of a Germanic epic that was written in Anglo-Saxon in about 800. (p. 207)

11.   What made learning remain the monopoly of a specially trained elite in the West? (p. 207)

12.   What were the particularly Germanic and Celtic decorative styles that influenced the visual arts in the Middle Ages? (p. 207)

REVIEW AND ANTICIPATION

1. Review the economic disruptions of the Roman Empire during the third and fourth centuries. Do you think the decentralization of authority under the Merovingians merely continued that trend or was something new?

2. Of the roles that the Church began to take on in the sixth century, which do you think will have the most impact in the future? Which do you think will be most controversial?

Chapter 16
The First Europe:
The Carolingian Age, 750-900

OVERVIEW

For a century and a half, it appeared that Europe would be united again under a unified system. Carolingian kings on the Continent assembled a restored political unit, and Anglo-Saxon kings moved toward centralized authority.

1. The Rise of the Carolingians. The family of the Carolingians became increasingly powerful under the reign of the Merovingians. They took control of the office of Mayor of the Palace and virtually ruled the country. They strengthened the military and successfully defended the borders. They encouraged the Church and its missionary activities. Finally, with support of the popes, Pépin deposed the Merovingian king and took the crown himself. The Carolingians increased their ties to the papacy and granted land in Italy to the popes.

2. The Reign of Charlemagne, 768-814. Charlemagne's military skill allowed him to form a large kingdom that extended from Spain to Germany and Italy. He expanded the concept of kingship so that he ruled closely over a Christian society. His rule was highly personal, and the administration he established depended heavily on personal ties of loyalty. He reformed the Church, and his close ties with the papacy culminated in 800, when he received the title of emperor.

3. The Carolingian Renaissance. Charlemagne believed that a rejuvenated, well-ordered state depended upon well educated leaders. He encouraged a revival of learning by establishing a palace school to which he brought scholars from all over Europe. His scholars established sound educational methods, corrected old texts, revised handwriting so it would be more legible, established scriptoria where texts could be copied. These efforts caused a cultural flowering and generated many influential works.

4. The Disintegration of the Carolingian Empire. Charlemagne's empire dissolved from internal and external pressures. Internally, the kingdom was divided among Charlemagne's grandsons in the Germanic tradition, which increased internal warfare and strengthened the independence of powerful vassals. Further pressure came from outside invaders: Moslems, Hungarians, and especially Scandinavians, who put so much pressure on the centralized authority that local government became more powerful.

5.   <u>Anglo-Saxon England</u>. In the late sixth century, the Anglo-Saxons converted to Christianity, subsequently stimulating a cultural revival in England. Vikings conquered a portion of England, but by the tenth century Anglo-Saxon kings were able to reestablish their kingdom. Their strong organization built on tight local administrative units would ultimately lead to England's distinctive constitutional system.

MAP EXERCISE

See map on p. 74.

1.   Locate the following regions: Saxony, Papal States, Danelaw, Wessex, Brittany. Locate the following cities: London, York, Canterbury, Aachen, Tours, Rome, Ravenna.

2.   In what city did Charlemagne establish his capital? What area of England was taken by Scandinavians?

3.   Notice the extent of Charlemagne's territory. What areas do you think his successors will have most difficulty holding? Why?

4.   Locate the main external foes of the Carolingians: Northmen, Slavs, Moslems. Which posed the greatest threat?

5.   Draw lines on the map showing the division of Charlemagne's empire by the Treaty of Verdun. (Consult Map 16.2 in your text). Of the three resulting kingdoms, which do you think would be the strongest? Why?

STUDY QUESTIONS

1.   How did the Carolingians manage to depose the Merovingians? What role did the Church play in this? Why was the Church's role important?

2.   What kind of military innovations did the Carolingians develop? How did they raise the money for new armies?

3.   What was Charlemagne's concept of kingship? Do you think his accepting the title of emperor was the logical outcome of his concept? Why or why not? How did Charlemagne view the title? What's your evidence?

4.   How did Charlemagne's concept of kingship involve him in church reform? What reforms did he initiate?

MAP 16.1 The Empire of Charlemagne

5.   What was the administrative organization of Charlemagne's empire? In what way did this administration depend upon the personal loyalty of vassals and the personal strength of Charlemagne? How did this organization fail under Charlemagne's successors?

6.   What was the educational philosophy developed in Charlemagne's court? What kind of educational reforms did this philosophy generate?

7.   In what fields did Carolingian scholars produce their work? Who were some of the famous scholars attached to this court, and what was their contribution?

8.   What caused the disintegration of the Carolingian Empire? What groups were strengthened during this disintegration?

9.   What impact did the Viking invasions have on Anglo-Saxon England? What state formed the center for Anglo-Saxon resistance to the Vikings?

10.   Describe the political organization of the Anglo-Saxon kingdom. What made this organization more effective than that of the Carolingians?

IDENTIFICATION

TRY TO USE EACH OF THESE TERMS AT LEAST ONCE IN ANSWERING THE STUDY QUESTIONS AND MAP EXERCISES

*Charles Martel	*Pépin the Short	*Battle of Tours
Boniface	Donation of	Donation of Pépin
benefice	Constantine	*Charlemagne
ministerial kingship	*missi*	*scriptoria*
*Treaty of Verdun	Alcuin	*Louis the Pious
Witan	*Alfred the Great	*fyrd*
Saracens	shire	Lombards
	Magyars	Danelaw

CHRONOLOGY

List in chronological order the words in the Identification section that have an asterisk (*). As you list these items, put a circle around those that are contemporary.

SAMPLE QUESTIONS

1.   What was the significance of the Battle of Tours? (p. 210)

2.   When people received a benefice from the Carolingian kings, what did they owe in return? (p. 210)

3.   What is the relationship between the Donation of Pépin and the Donation of Constantine? (p. 212)

4.   What kind of things did Charlemagne do to expand the bonds of loyalty of his powerful subjects? (p. 214)

5.   What title did Charlemagne acquire in 800? (p. 215)

6.   What were the liberal arts that formed the educational system of the Carolingians? (p. 216)

7.   What steps did Charlemagne take to spread his educational reform beyond his own palace school? (p. 216)

8.   What architectural style influenced the Carolingian churches, and how does that style express Charlemagne's political philosophy? (p. 217)

9.   What were the provisions of the Treaty of Verdun? (p. 218)

10.   What impact did the Viking invasions have on England? (p. 221)

11.   What elements of Anglo-Saxon tradition made local authority important? (p. 221)

REVIEW AND ANTICIPATION

1.   Review Germanic culture and values. What elements were continued by the Carolingians?

2.   Review the administrative structure established by Octavian. Contrast that with Charlemagne's empire. Could Charlemagne have introduced similar elements?

3.   Charlemagne's concept of kingship placed him in charge of the church and the papacy. Do you think the popes will continue to accept that hierarchy or will this be disputed?

4.   Do you think the differences in these early forms of administration of France and England will lead to long-term differences in the two? In what ways do you expect them to develop differently?

Chapter 17
Lordship and Dependency:
Feudalism and Manorialism

OVERVIEW

The disintegration of the Carolingian Empire created a fragmentation of political society that strengthened local authority and dramatically increased the power of local lords. Within this structure new forms of order developed that established the relationships between people that would shape the subsequent few centuries.

1. Lordship and Dependency. As effective central governments broke down, power became privatized and concentrated in the hands of landowners. These lords established new relationships that essentially bound all members of society together in some form of dependent relationship. Nobles were bound to lords and served as a fighting force in exchange for a livelihood, while peasants were bound to their manors.

2. The Community of the Powerful: The Feudal Order. The nobility were bound in contractual dependency ties. These relationships gave lords and their vassals mutual rights and responsibilities that theoretically linked society's nobility into a hierarchy. In reality, many of these mutual rights led to conflict and required warfare to enforce them. This system created a complex way of life in which family ties were central, marriages arranged, with life crudely focused on the creation of competent warriors.

3. The Community of the Servile: Manorialism. Lords evolved a system by which they could govern and exploit to their benefit the agricultural laborers on their estates. The fiefs were divided into self-sufficient manors, with agricultural fields, woodlands, and pastures, complete with villages of serfs. The serfs were bound to the land, but had the protection of custom. The serf owed the lord labor and goods, but in return gained a place in a close-knit community and the use of a plot of land sufficient to support him and his family.

4. The Christian Community in the World of Lordship and Dependency. The religious establishment also became caught up in the system of lordship and dependency. This caused some corruption in the Church as ecclesiastical officials became vassals and lords with all the obligations and rights attendant to that relationship. However, in addition, this system allowed the Church to become involved in more aspects of medieval secular life, attempting, for example, to alleviate some of the violence of medieval life, and adding Christian principles to the warrior code.

STUDY QUESTIONS

1.   Describe the rights and responsibilities of both vassals and lords. How did the ceremony of homage, fealty, and investiture symbolically reflect this contractual relationship?

2.   What values were generated by these feudal ties? How was family life organized in order to forward it?

3.   Describe the medieval manor. What components did it contain? How were the agricultural fields usually laid out? What were the woods and common pasture lands used for?

4.   What obligations did serfs owe their lords? What rights did serfs have? Where would a serf appeal if he/she felt his/her rights were being violated?

5.   How did ecclesiastical involvement in the system of lordship and dependency lead to corruption in the Church? How did churchmen attempt to influence the system for the better?

6.   In what way did the systems of dependency facilitate a spectacular period of growth in society and culture?

IDENTIFICATION

TRY TO USE EACH OF THESE TERMS AT LEAST ONCE IN ANSWERING THE STUDY QUESTIONS

feudalism	commendation	vassal
lord	benefice	fief
homage	fealty	investiture
seigneurial system	subinfeudation	demesne
mansi	stewards	baillifs
serf	Peace of God	Truce of God
open-field system	two-field system	

SAMPLE QUESTIONS

1.   What is a benefice (or fief), and what part did it play in establishing the feudal order? (p. 226)

2.   The feudal contract called for the vassal to pay aids (special payments) under certain circumstances. What were some of these circumstances? (p. 227)

3. Describe the process of subinfeudation. (p. 227)

4. What legal provision allowed women to exert some control and influence over the lands their husbands could control? (p. 229)

5. What is the difference between a serf and a vassal? (pp. 225, 231)

6. What is the two-field system of agriculture? (p. 229)

7. What usually served as a check to prevent lords from being too oppressive to their serfs? (p. 231)

8. What recreational pleasures did serfs have as part of their community life? (p. 232)

9. Clerical writers established a theoretical social structure of medieval society based on what three orders? (p. 233)

10. What steps did churchmen take to attempt to alleviate violence in medieval society? (p. 233)

REVIEW AND ANTICIPATION

1. Review the Germanic values as expressed in early Merovingian society. In what ways does the feudal contract continue and build on these values? In what ways was the way of life similar?

2. Review the three cultural units that emerged from the fall of the Roman Empire. Which was most advanced by the eighth century? Why?

3. Feudalism is based on mutual rights and responsibilities in a contract. Do you think the contractual nature of this bond will lead to a growing emphasis on law and lawyers in this society?

Chapter 18
Economic and Social Revival, 1000-1300

OVERVIEW

After 1000, agricultural improvement spurred a dramatic economic growth that stimulated social change throughout society.

1. <u>Population Growth.</u> Between 900 and 1350, population in western Europe approximately doubled. This may have been caused by less disease and warfare, more food, or even increased psychological well-being. Whatever its cause, such demographic change affected all aspects of society.

2. <u>Agricultural Expansion.</u> Increased agricultural production was the foundation without which economic expansion could not have occurred. This increase was caused by many factors: improved climate, new land clearance, technological advances, improved methods of tillage, and, no doubt, human ingenuity. One aspect of this agricultural expansion was colonization on Europe's frontiers.

3. <u>The Revival of Trade and Manufacturing.</u> Agricultural expansion stimulated the growth of commerce and manufacturing in western Europe. Italian city-states began to draw on the Mediterranean trade previously dominated by the Byzantines and Moslems. Scandinavians established another trade route from the Baltic Sea to Constantinople. Local trade increased, too, and stimulated manufacturing by skilled artisans and cottage industries, particularly in cloth manufacturing.

4. <u>Economic Consequences of Increased Production.</u> The new economic activity worked to transform the old early medieval rural pattern of life. Cities grew and attracted population. More money came into circulation allowing people to produce for profits rather than self-sufficiency.

5. <u>Social Change: The Bourgeoisie.</u> Economic growth saw the emergence of a new social group, the middle class. This group was based in cities and constantly sought the kinds of freedoms that would allow them to pursue trade. Their efforts yielded a number of freedoms for towns, facilitating the development of structures for self-government. They developed business innovations to accommodate their needs, became stratified according to wealth, and persecuted Jews, who previously had dominated the commercial market.

6. <u>Social Change: The Nobility.</u> Between 1000 and 1300 while the nobility remained the dominant social group, it underwent transformations. To

preserve wealth, only eldest sons could inherit, reducing the position of women in the family. Material conditions improved, leading to more displays of luxury and the development of a code of conduct that defined nobility and the relationship between the genders.

7.   Social Change: The Peasantry. In many parts of western Europe in the twelfth and thirteenth centuries serfs were freed to become tenant farmers. Due to this, many peasants were able to gain increased prosperity, but most continued to be exploited and remained at the bottom of the social scale.

MAP EXERCISE

See map on p. 82.

1.   Locate the following cities: Constantinople, Kiev, Novgorod, Copenhagen, Paris, Genoa, Venice, Pisa, Bruges, Antwerp, London.

2.   Which Italian city dominated the trade in the eastern Mediterranean? Which cities dominated the trade in the western Mediterranean?

3.   What routes was Copenhagen well suited to exploit?

4.   To where did the English export most of their wool for production?

STUDY QUESTIONS

1.   What technological advances and new methods of tillage and animal husbandry helped increase agricultural production after 1000? What specific advantages were there in a three-field (instead of two-field) system of crop rotation?

2.   What were the trade items that were most important in the long-distance trade from the Mediterranean? Where did international traders display their wares?

3.   How did a shift to a money economy change the nature of agricultural production and people's attitudes toward work? Do you think people were motivated to work harder before the growth of a money economy or after? Which way is closer to our system?

4.   What freedoms did the bourgeoisie seek as they developed commerce and manufacturing? How and to what degree did they achieve these freedoms? How were their personal lives more free than those of the rural populations? Did women share in this increased freedom?

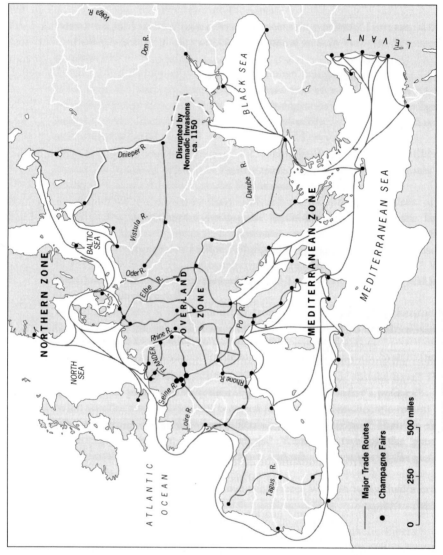

MAP 18.1 Trade Routes, Twelfth and Thirteenth Centuries

5. Describe the purpose and organization of guilds. Do we have any comparable institutions now?

6. How did the position of Jews in western Europe deteriorate as the bourgeoisie came into increasing prominence?

7. What business innovations developed as the bourgeoisie developed their commercial interests? Which remain central to our society today?

8. What was the code of chivalry? How did it transform the behavior of the nobility? How did it affect women?

9. What are the different positions in the argument on the origins of the medieval nobility? Why is it important to understand how the nobility were established?

10. What improvements did some peasants gain as a result of all these economic changes?

IDENTIFICATION

TRY TO USE EACH OF THESE TERMS AT LEAST ONCE IN ANSWERING THE STUDY QUESTIONS AND MAP EXERCISES

three-field system	Champagne fairs	cottage industry
bourgeoisie	charter	communes
guilds	apprentice	journeyman
master	chivalry	tournaments

SAMPLE QUESTIONS

1. What were some possible causes for the population growth that began about 900? (p. 237)

2. What technological innovations spurred the increased productivity after A.D. 1000? (pp. 237-238)

3. What were the chief areas of new colonization after 1000? (p. 237)

4. What new sources of power (instead of the traditional human with ox) began to be extensively used after 1000? (p. 238)

5. What were the principal trade items that were brought from Central Asia and China? (p. 239)

6.   Where were the large fairs held that were the meeting place of international traders? (p. 239)

7.   Where was the main region to which English farmers exported wool for its production into cloth? (p. 240)

8.   What factors lured merchants and artisans to old administrative centers? (p. 242)

9.   How did lords change their relationships to their serfs in response to the growing money economy? (p. 242)

10.   What was the difference between a town with a limited charter and a commune? (p. 243)

11.   For what purpose were guilds organized? (p. 244)

12.   In what ways was the code of chivalry supposed to modify warfare? (p. 246)

13.   When serfs were freed, what did their status become? (p. 248)

REVIEW AND ANTICIPATION

1.   Review the traditional manorial organization in the early Middle Ages. What change do you think will have the greatest impact?

2.   Of the changes described here, which do you think will have the largest impact in breaking down the medieval way of life?

3.   Which social groups do you expect to become a revolutionary force in the Middle Ages? Why?

Chapter 19
The Restoration of Political Order:
The Revival of Monarchy, 1000-1300

OVERVIEW

By 1300, some rulers were able to restore centralized control and begin to build institutional forms to sustain it. This chapter considers the restored states in Germany and Italy (collectively known as the Holy Roman Empire), England, and France.

1. The Holy Roman Empire. The decentralization that occurred after the fall of the Carolingian Empire was first reversed in central Europe in an area that came to be called the Holy Roman Empire. In the tenth century, Otto I succeeded in establishing a German kingdom and exerting royal control over portions of Italy. He was crowned Holy Roman Emperor. This centralizing tendency was resisted by various forces: During the inverstiture controversy, the Church gained more independence, local lords benefited from the struggle to gain more sovereignty, and Italian city-states were able to play one side against the other and become more independent. There were times when emperors like Frederick I were able to restore more unified authority or like Frederick II attempted to establish a centralized state in Sicily. In spite of the resistance to centralized authority, for centuries the Holy Roman Empire remained the most prominent state in western Europe.

2. England. In 1066, England was conquered by William of Normandy, who was able then to impose a tight feudal organization over a unified land. His successors were able to establish a strong fiscal base and created royal servants and courts who served as effective elements of central administration. Particularly significant was the growth of royal courts as a way of centralizing authority. Kings were not able to rule absolutely, however. In their attempts to exert royal control, they clashed with traditional rights of the nobility, who were able to reassert those rights. England then developed along a model of a strong monarchy that ruled under limits. This model was expressed in the growth of parliament.

3. France. The centralization of France proceeded slowly because local barons were very powerful. Only in the twelfth century could the Capetian kings begin to use rights implicit in the feudal contract to expand control over their powerful neighboring vassals. They also developed institutions that allowed them to govern their realm effectively: full-time royal administrators, new taxation policies, convening the Estates General. They were successful enough to be able to challenge papal power in the beginning of the fourteenth century and win.

STUDY QUESTIONS

1.   Contrast the theoretical bases that the following emperors used to attempt to exert centralized control: Otto I, Frederick I, Frederick II. Which was most successful in his own time? Which do you think will be the most successful model for the future?

2.   What were the issues in the investiture struggle? Who were the main parties involved? How was it resolved? What were the main results of this prolonged struggle?

3.   What made it easier for the English kings to centralize their authority as compared to their German and French contemporaries?

4.   What legal reforms and innovations did the English kings develop in expanding the use of royal courts as a way of exerting their authority?

5.   What events/documents/institutions occurred in England that guaranteed that the kings, however powerful, were not above the law?

6.   What was significant about the Model Parliament in broadening English representation? How was the Estates General organized differently from the English Parliament? Which model do you think would give most effective broad representation to the people?

7.   Describe the fragmentation of France and the consolidation of local principalities prior to the emergence of a centralized monarchy. What means did the Capetian kings ultimately use to consolidate their territory?

8.   What kinds of administrative innovations did the French kings establish to centralize their government?

IDENTIFICATION

TRY TO USE EACH OF THESE TERMS AT LEAST ONCE IN ANSWERING THE STUDY QUESTIONS

*Otto I	*Edward I	*Innocent III
*Henry IV	Welfs (Guelfs)	*Henry II
Hohenstaufens	Capetians	*John I
*Frederick I	*Louis IX	*Model Parliament
*Frederick II	lay investiture	*Eleanor of Aquitaine
Domesday Book	College of Cardinals	*Philip IV
*Thomas à Becket	Lombard League	*Gregory VII

investiture struggle   *Louis VI   *Concordat of Worms
Peace of Constance   grand jury   *Magna Carta
*William I

CHRONOLOGY

List in chronological order the words in the Identification section that have an asterisk
(*). As you list these items, put a circle around those that are contemporary.

SAMPLE QUESTIONS

1. What did Otto I use to strengthen the institutional base for royal power? (p. 251)

2. After 1059, how were popes selected? (p. 254)

3. What did the Peace of Constance guarantee for Italian cities? (p. 255)

4. In the twelfth-century struggle between Frederick I and the papacy, from where (groups/regions) did the papacy draw its support? (p. 255)

5. What were some of the results of the Norman conquest of England? (pp. 257-258)

6. What were the issues that caused the clash between Henry II and Thomas à Becket? (pp. 259-260)

7. In what crucial areas did the Magna Carta curb royal power? (p. 260)

8. What was the political significance of the failure of the marriage of Eleanor to Louis VII and her subsequent marriage to Henry II of England? (p. 262)

9. What were the three "estates" represented in the Estates General of France? (p. 264)

10. What was the role of the French *baillis* (bailiffs)? (p. 263)

REVIEW AND ANTICIPATION

1. Review the policy toward church/state relationship outlined by Ambrose and Pope Gelasius. Do you think their position is closer to that of Gregory VII or Henry IV (and his father Henry III)?

2.   Review the elements of Germanic law. What reforms of the English court system most transformed the old legal principles?

3.   At the beginning of the fourteenth century, both the English king and the French king claimed authority over the valuable lands in southern France. Do you expect this to cause trouble? Do you think it will be easily resolved?

Chapter 20
The Medieval Expansion of Europe, 1000-1300

OVERVIEW

After 1000, western Europe began to grow more prosperous and expand, spreading religion and commerce, and challenging by force of arms the Moslem world in Spain, southern Italy, and the Holy Land.

1. Missionary Expansion. In the late tenth and eleventh centuries, the Christian West converted the Scandinavian countries. Then Christianity spread eastward into the Slavic lands, and with less success as far east as the Mongol Empire and China.

2. Colonization and Commercial Expansion. Western Europeans were motivated to expand by commerce as well as religion. Germans established settlements in eastern Europe and Vikings established the first state in Russia. Italian merchants moved beyond the Mediterranean world to trade with Asia and down to the coast of Africa.

3. Military Expansion in Spain and Southern Italy. By the eleventh century, Christian kings in northern Spain were able to begin to reconquer the Spanish territory that had been controlled by Moslems. By 1300 the Christians had conquered all but Granada, and the kingdoms had established many of the centralizing institutions that marked the northern kingdoms. The Normans had begun incursions into southern Italy. Soon the papacy recognized this as a Norman kingdom. It was later taken over by the Hohenstaufens, and remained a fertile area of cultural exchange between Christians, Byzantines and Moslems.

4. Military Expansion: The Crusades. In the eleventh century, a weakened Byzantine Empire was threatened by a strengthened Moslem world. The emperor asked for help from the pope, and a crusade was called. Crusading armies were able to establish a Christian kingdom in the Holy Land, but it was precarious. Further crusades were called to try to hold the territory, but in 1291 the last Christian stronghold was taken by the Moslems. In the process, Christians alienated the Byzantines, even conquering the capital of the empire for a while.

MAP EXERCISE

See map of Christian expansion in Iberia on p. 91.

1.   On the map of the Iberian peninsula, locate the following kingdoms: Portugal, León-Castile, Aragon, Granada. Which one is in a position to become the most powerful? Why?

2.   On the map of the Iberian peninsula, locate the following cities: Toledo, Granada, Lisbon. Which of these do you think is most important for strategic control of the peninsula? Which is best situated to lead in maritime exploration?

See map of the early crusades on p. 92.

3.   On the map of Europe, mark the areas that were Roman Catholic, Greek Orthodox and the crusader kingdoms in the East. Which cities in the crusader kingdoms do you think will be most vulnerable to attack? Which do you think will be the last to fall?

4.   On the map of Europe, mark the route of the First Crusade and of the Third Crusade. What are the advantages and disadvantages of each route?

STUDY QUESTIONS

1.   Both missionary zeal and the drive for profits spurred Europeans beyond their immediate borders. To what regions did western Europeans go in each of these pursuits? Which motive proved most effective in "Europeanizing" the people they encountered?

2.   Describe the progress of the Reconquista. What kingdoms were involved, and what were the key events until 1300?

3.   What kind of political organization developed in the kingdoms that were established as a result of the Reconquest? How did the nobles and townspeople restrict royal rule?

4.   How was the kingdom of Sicily established? What had happened to it by 1300?

5.   What were the motivations of the people involved in the First Crusade? What did the pope expect? What did the Byzantine emperor expect? What did the crusaders expect? Who was most disappointed?

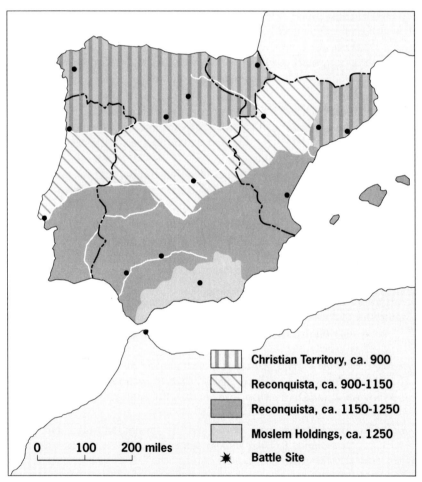

Map 20.1 Christian Expansion in Iberia

Christian Territory, ca. 900

Reconquista, ca. 900-1150

Reconquista, ca. 1150-1250

Moslem Holdings, ca. 1250

0   100   200 miles

Battle Site

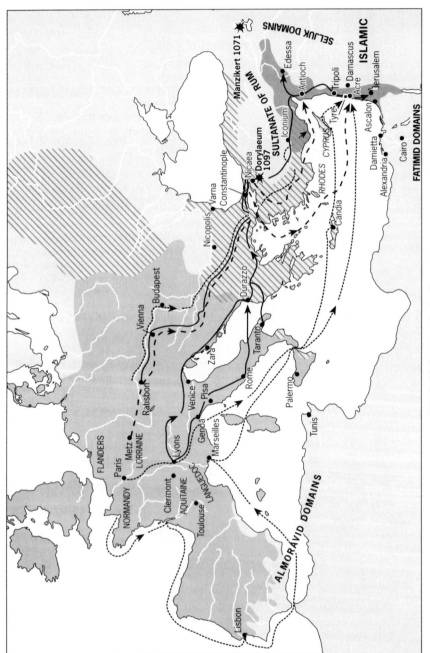

MAP 20.2 The Early Crusades

6.   After the First Crusade, the rest were less successful. What did the Fourth Crusade do that caused much disillusionment with the crusading ideal?

7.   What actions did the crusaders take to try to defend the Holy Land? Which do you think was the most effective?

8.   What were the results of the Crusades?

IDENTIFICATION

TRY TO USE EACH OF THESE TERMS AT LEAST ONCE IN ANSWERING THE STUDY QUESTIONS AND MAP EXERCISES

*Marco Polo	Reconquista	Moors
Granada	Cortes	*Roger II
Song of Roland	*The Cid*	Seljuk Turks
*Alexius	*Urban II	Outremer
Comnenus	*Louis IX	*Genghis Khan
*Saladin	Knights	Teutonic Knights
Knights Templar	Hospitaler	*Latin Empire of
*Fatimids	*Abbasids	Constantinople

CHRONOLOGY

List in chronological order the words in the Identification section that have an asterisk (*). As you list these items, put a circle around those that are contemporary.

SAMPLE QUESTIONS

1.   What peoples were converted to Christianity in the late tenth and eleventh centuries? (p. 268)

2.   What peoples established settlements that constituted the first effective state in Russia? (p. 268)

3.   What events occurred in the Moslem world in the early eleventh century that facilitated the progress of the Reconquest? (p. 269)

4.   What two vernacular literary works celebrated the feats of Christian warriors against the Moors? (p. 269)

5.   What caused the decline of the Kingdom of Sicily? (p. 271)

6.   What happened at the battle of Manzikert? (p. 271)

7.   What pope called the First Crusade? (p. 272)

8.   What actions ended any hope for collaboration between Byzantines and crusaders? (p. 275)

9.   What threat caused Christians and Moslems to ally for a while in the mid-thirteenth century? (p. 276)

REVIEW AND ANTICIPATION

1.   Review the ways the nobles restricted royal power in England in the early thirteenth century. What similar process occurred in the Spanish kingdoms, and what institution developed there to limit royal power?

2.   Review the social changes that accompanied the population growth after 1000. Which of these do you think helped stimulate western Europeans to go on crusade?

3.   How do you think the experience of centuries of crusade against "nonbelievers" will influence Spanish actions when they go to the New World and confront new pagans?

Chapter 21
Religious Renewal, 1000-1300

OVERVIEW

A central event during this period was a religious renewal that challenged some traditional assumptions about religion and engaged both the greatest minds and the deepest passions of people. Its result was to bind Europeans into a unified Christian civilization.

1. The Origins of the Reform Movement. In the tenth century, the Church seemed badly in need of reform. It had become controlled by lay lords, and religious leaders too often seemed worldly and corrupt. The origin of the reform movement came from monasteries, but the reform sprang from three sources: the popes, trying to free the Church from secular control, monasteries, seeking spiritual perfection, and the people, looking for new outlets for religious expression.

2. Papal Reform: The Quest for Order and Uniformity. In their attempt to set up a hierarchy that would represent a reformed church, the popes increased the centralized administrative system of the papacy that effectively connected all of Europe to the pope. Religious law was codified and became another effective centralizing force. Finally, religious dogma was standardized and interpreted in a way that made the clergy a central part of all Christians' lives.

3. Monastic Reform: Spiritual Seeking. As the papacy regulated organization and practice, monasteries were in the forefront of seeking new spiritual dimensions. Instead of just seeing God as a wrathful judge, some looked for ways to join the human spirit to a loving divinity. New monastic orders were founded that offered new paths to spirituality. The Cluniacs emphasized sacred rites; Carthusians stressed solitary prayer; Cistercians emphasized labor, simplicity of life and contemplation. Crusading orders fought in armies of God. Perhaps most influential were the Franciscans and Dominicans who emphasized poverty and preaching and who worked in the world instead of retreating behind monastery walls.

4. Popular Reform: Enthusiasm, Dissent, Heresy. New, passionate religious feelings were also expressed by common people. New intensity was given to veneration of saints and to pilgrimages. Popular preachers, praising poverty and criticizing the wealth of the clergy, drew large followings. Some groups went beyond what the Church could accept as dissent and were declared heretics. Two such groups were the Waldensians, who believed that priests and sacraments were unimportant and that one only needed to imitate

Christ's life, and the Cathari, who were dualists. The Cathari were eliminated by crusade, and the Church established the Inquisition to stamp out such dissenters.

5.   <u>Consequences of the Medieval Religious Revival.</u> The medieval reformation strengthened the religious organization, redefined the relationship between church and state, stimulated intellectual and artistic production, and broadened the range of spiritual possibilities. However, it may also have created a structure that would cause some people to strive for even greater reform.

STUDY QUESTIONS

1.   How did the popes concentrate authority in their hands? What kinds of administrative institutions did they establish to implement this concentrated authority? At whose expense was this increased power won?

2.   Why did churchmen believe it necessary to undertake a codification of the law of the Church? What impact did such codification have on the power of the Church?

3.   What kinds of clarification of doctrine took place in the twelfth and thirteenth centuries? Which of the new decrees do you think would be most influential in increasing the importance of the clergy in everyone's life?

4.   Contrast the religious emphasis among the following monastic orders: Cluniacs, Cistercians, Carthusians. What was each trying to do? Which do you think would be most influential on people around them? Why?

5.   Contrast the prevailing religious mentality before 1000 with that which was developing after. How do the figures illustrating this chapter reveal these changing views? Which is most consistent with modern Christian churches?

6.   Compare and contrast the Dominicans and the Franciscans. What elements do they share that make both influential forces in society? What social group do you think would be more influenced by the Dominicans and which by the Franciscans?

7.   What dissenting and heretical groups emphasized the importance of poverty in seeking spirituality? Why was this emphasis particularly threatening to the Church? What saved the Franciscans from being declared heretics?

8.   What were the beliefs of the Cathari? What was it about their life that made them appealing to common people? What happened to their movement?

9.   What were the results of the religious reform movement? Which do you think was the most important during the Middle Ages? Which do you think was the most enduring?

IDENTIFICATION

TRY TO USE EACH OF THESE TERMS AT LEAST ONCE IN ANSWERING THE STUDY QUESTIONS

decretals	papal *curia*	College of Cardinals
legates	diocese	*Decretum*
canon law	*Gratian	penance
sacraments	transubstantiation	Cistercian order
Cluniac order	Carthusian order	Franciscans
*Bernard of Clairvaux	Dominicans	*Children's Crusade
*Arnold of Brescia	*Francis of Assisi	Cathari
Albigensian heresy	Waldensian heresy	
	Inquisition	

CHRONOLOGY

List in chronological order the words in the Identification section that have an asterisk (*). As you list these items, put a circle around those that are contemporary.

SAMPLE QUESTIONS

1.   What was the role of papal legates? (p. 281)

2.   From what sources did popes gain a constantly increasing income? (p. 281)

3.   What is a sacrament, and how many were established in the thirteenth century? (p. 282)

4.   What is transubstantiation? (p. 283)

5.   What influential Cistercian emphasized active participation in worldly life? (p. 286)

6.   The military orders (i.e., Templars) were involved in holy war. Their activities in the Holy Land led them into what other activities that brought them great wealth? (p. 287)

7.   Which of the mendicant orders was most involved in the universities? (p. 287)

8.   Why was anticlericalism so often a part of popular religious reform? (p. 289)

9.   What belief caused the Cathari to repudiate the God of the Old Testament? (p. 290)

10.   What special legal techniques was the Inquisition empowered to employ to identify suspected heretics? (p. 290)

REVIEW AND ANTICIPATION

1.   Review how the kings of England in the twelfth century increased their power by taking control of the legal system through royal courts. Do you think the pope's increasing reliance on canon law is a comparable centralizing force? In what ways do you think control of law is an effective way of controlling society?

2.   The Church established absolute rules about what people were supposed to believe (like transubstantiation). How do you think people will react to such increased rigidity of doctrine?

3.   Over what particular issues do you expect criticism of the Church to continue?

Chapter 22
Intellectual and Artistic Revival,
1000-1300

OVERVIEW

During this time there was an upsurge in creative activity in all fields. In the twelfth century, there was a burst of creative experimentation. In the thirteenth century, there was an emphasis on summarizing and synthesizing knowledge. There was also a split in the general cultural life: Learned people wrote in Latin, but others used vernacular languages increasingly as vehicles of creative expression.

1. The World of Learning: Education. With the growth of courtly and religious administration, education opened career opportunities, so educational opportunities expanded. Monastery and cathedral schools taught students Latin and the seven liberal arts. About 1200, the first universities were established and, like towns, gained charters that gave them corporate rights, including the right to grant degrees. Teaching methods were developed that emphasized texts and logic, and university communities became more complex, often generating resentment in the towns in which they were located.

2. The World of Learning: The Medieval "Sciences." Medieval thinkers organized knowledge into interrelated segments, called "sciences." The most prestigious was theology (including philosophy). In this science the greatest thinkers applied logic to religious truths to reconcile seeming contradictions and to come to a fuller understanding of God's universe. This enterprise was greatly advanced by the rediscovery of Greek texts, particularly previously unknown works by Aristotle. Thomas Aquinas was the most successful at reconciling revelation and reason. A second important science was the study of law (and human society). This involved the reclamation of Roman law and reflections upon the nature of the state. The third science, that of the natural world, was least important in the Middle Ages. However, in the thirteenth century some people (especially among the Franciscans) argued that the study of the natural world by observation was important. This set the stage for future scientific endeavors.

3. Beyond the Learned World: Vernacular Literature. Literature began to be composed in the language of the people primarily for a courtly audience. There were various kinds of vernacular literature: epics, love poetry, romances (that combined love with adventure), dramas, and amusing folk tales. Probably the greatest of these authors was Dante Alighieri who expressed the range of human experience.

4.   In All Worlds: The Visual Arts. Two styles of church architecture dominated this period, Romanesque and Gothic. The Romanesque was a product of the monastic world and the Gothic of the growing cities. Each had its own architectural style, and both served as vehicles for the expression of the other visual arts.

5.   The Underlying Spirit of Medieval Culture. Uniting all these intellectual endeavors were two seemingly contradictory impulses: a search for truth beyond human existence and a sympathetic appreciation for humankind.

STUDY QUESTIONS

1.   Describe the curriculum and teaching methods of medieval universities. What skills were specifically cultivated by this method of teaching? How did the organization of Thomas Aquinas' *Summa Theologica* reflect the university teaching method?

2.   How were universities organized? What degrees did they grant? What was their relationship with the surrounding region? Do you think the independence granted them was important in fostering knowledge?

3.   What thinkers attempted to use logic to resolve religious questions? What were some of their ideas? Who was most successful in this enterprise?

4.   Describe the two approaches to theological truths embodied by the Averroist and the Platonic-Augustinian traditions.

5.   What stimulated a revived interest in Roman law? Do you expect this to form as powerful a tool for kings as canon law did for popes?

6.   In what fields did natural sciences make the most advances? What Franciscans were most significant in its development?

7.   What were the most important medieval epics, and what did they try to do? How were the romances different from epics?

8.   What new values did the troubadours introduce into medieval society? What view of women did they express? To what degree are those values still held today?

9.   Who wrote plays in a classical model? How did medieval drama develop?

10.   Contrast the architectural styles of Romanesque and Gothic. In addition to the architectural features, what visual arts did each encourage?

11.   What are the two seemingly contradictory impulses in medieval thinking? Give two examples of each of the works discussed in this chapter that illustrate each of these impulses. Which do you think will have the greatest long-term impact?

IDENTIFICATION

TRY TO USE EACH OF THESE TERMS AT LEAST ONCE IN ANSWERING THE STUDY QUESTIONS

trivium	quadrivium	*disputatio*
college	dialectic	*Anselm of Bec
*Peter Abélard	Héloïse	*Peter Lombard
Scholastics	Averroists	*Bonaventura
*Thomas Aquinas	*Summa Theologica*	*Robert Grosseteste
*Roger Bacon	*chanson de geste*	troubadour
romance	Chrétien de Troyes	Gottfried von
*Geoffrey Chaucer	Hrotsvitha	Strasbourg
*Dante Alighieri	*Romanesque	*Gothic
flying buttresses	*fabliaux*	
*Wolfram von		
Eschenbach		

CHRONOLOGY

List in chronological order the words in the Identification section that have an asterisk (*). As you list these items, put a circle around those that are contemporary.

SAMPLE QUESTIONS

1.   Why was there an increasing demand for expanded education during the eleventh and twelfth centuries? (p. 294)

2.   Where were the earliest universities founded? (p. 295)

3.   Why was the lecture style of teaching so important at medieval universities? (p. 296)

4.   What is dialectic? (p. 297)

5.   What did Abélard believe that "truth" consists of? (p. 298)

6.   What became the basic text for teaching theology, and what teaching method did it standardize? (p. 298)

7.   What two paths to truth did Aquinas recognize and try to reconcile? (p. 299)

8.   What persuaded medieval thinkers to study nature? (p. 301)

9.   What are "vernacular languages"? (p. 301)

10.   For what audience was vernacular literature composed? (p. 302)

11.   What values were expressed in the *chanson de geste, Song of Roland*? (p. 302)

12.   Who wrote the *Divine Comedy*, and what themes does it develop? (p. 304)

13.   Where did Gothic churches first appear? (p. 307)

14.   What was the difference in sculptural style between works on Romanesque and Gothic churches? (p. 305, 307)

15.   In what way did church music become more complex by the thirteenth century? (p. 308)

REVIEW AND ANTICIPATION

1.   Review Neoplatonism in the late Roman Empire. What in this philosophy would discourage people from studying the natural world?

2.   Review the goals of the monastic reform at Cluny. What did they emphasize that made it likely that they would develop large ornate churches? Why didn't Cistercians or Carthusians develop large churches?

3.   Of the medieval "sciences," which will become most important in the future, and which will be eclipsed? Why do you think that will happen?

Chapter 23
Transition in Economic, Social, and Political Institutions, 1300-1500

OVERVIEW

By 1300, the expansion that had marked the previous two centuries of the medieval world came to an end. As a result of a series of tensions and troubles, the medieval world would be profoundly transformed.

1. Economic and Social Tensions and Readjustments. After 1300, the period of economic prosperity ended. Due to famine and disease, population dropped, bringing with it reduced commercial and industrial production. Landlords attempted to recoup losses by increasing pressure on peasantry, leading to peasant revolts. Cities were not immune to tension, and urban riots occurred as workers reacted to strict measures imposed by the wealthy trying to hold on to their position. An elite segment of the bourgeoisie amassed great fortunes and were in a position to take leadership as the economies reorganized.

2. Monarchy under Stress: France, England, Spain. The monarchies that were consolidating their authority during the central Middle Ages were confronted with a crisis during this century. France and England engaged in a Hundred Years' War that taxed their economies and triggered internal struggles. The French won the war and emerged in a strengthened position. The English faced a civil war after their loss, and only recovered their strong monarchy after the victory of Henry Tudor in the Wars of the Roses. The Spanish monarchies suffered internal warfare until the end of the period when the kingdoms of Castile and Aragon joined. By 1450, all three kingdoms had emerged from the crisis centralized again.

3. The Holy Roman Empire: The End of the Universal State. As other kingdoms were centralizing, the Holy Roman Empire further decentralized after 1250. The emperor was elected by seven princes, but he had no centralized authority, so the princes tended to act as sovereigns in their own lands. The emperor could no longer exert control over Italy. The northern Italian city-states became independent and tended to be run by strong individuals. The Papal States in the center also became more independent.

4. The Changing Scene in Eastern Europe and the Mediterranean World. In 1453, the Ottoman Turks captured Constantinople, ending the Byzantine Empire that had dominated in the East for 1000 years. They erected a centralized Moslem state that posed a threat to western Europe. A Polish state was established and Hungary continued to develop. The future power

in the area was the growing Russian state, whose ruler took the title tsar (caesar) claiming to be the heir of the Roman Empire.

MAP EXERCISE

1.   On the map of Central Europe and Western Asia ca. 1500, mark the following: Holy Roman Empire, Poland, Prussia, Hungary, Ukraine, Grand Principality of Moscow, Ottoman possessions by 1481.

2.   What countries will be most immediately threatened by the new Ottoman Empire?

3.   What countries will be most immediately threatened by the growing strength of Moscow? What countries will be threatened by the Holy Roman Empire?

STUDY QUESTIONS

1.   What was the impact of population decline on agricultural, commercial and industrial production? How did guilds and governments respond to these changes? Who benefited from their policies and who did not?

2.   What issues precipitated the outbreak of the Hundred Years' War? Who ultimately won? What was the result of the war in each country?

3.   What caused the Iberian kingdoms to delay the continuation of their reconquest during the fourteenth century? What finally resolved those problems?

4.   Describe the role of the Holy Roman Emperor after the issuance of the Golden Bull. What powers did the emperor lack that virtually defined the centralized monarchies of England, France, and Spain?

5.   What city-states dominated northern Italy? What form of government emerged there?

6.   What state conquered the Byzantine Empire? What was its organization? What was the major impact of this conquest on western Europe?

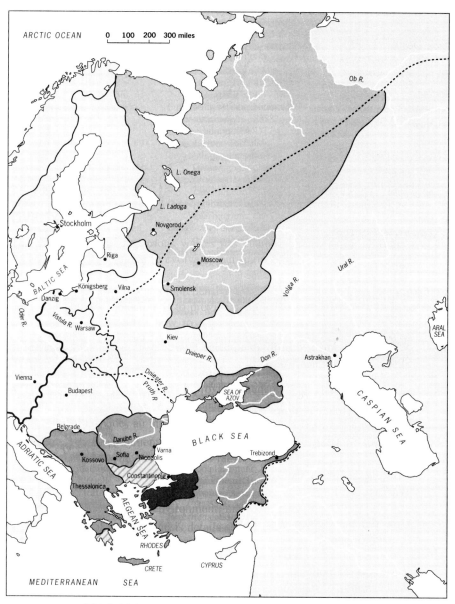

MAP 23.2 Central Europe and Western Asia, ca. 1500

IDENTIFICATION

TRY TO USE EACH OF THESE TERMS AT LEAST ONCE IN ANSWERING THE STUDY QUESTIONS AND MAP EXERCISES

Black Death	Janissaries	*Tamerlane
*Hundred Years' War	Ottoman Turks	*Henry V
*Henry VII	Istanbul	*Edward III
Medici	Golden Bull	sultan
Hanseatic League	*Jacquerie	*Wars of the Roses
*Joan of Arc	*Ferdinand & Isabella	

CHRONOLOGY

List in chronological order the words in the Identification section that have an asterisk (*). As you list these items, put a circle around those that are contemporary.

SAMPLE QUESTIONS

1.   What factors caused the population to fall after 1300? (p. 313)

2.   What policies did craft guilds adopt that reduced industrial productivity? (p. 314)

3.   What fields remained profitable during this time allowing some families to amass great fortunes? (p. 315)

4.   In what ways did parliament gain more power from the king of England during the Hundred Years' War? (p. 317)

5.   What role did Joan of Arc play in the Hundred Years' War? (p. 319)

6.   How did the French monarchy emerge strengthened after the Hundred Years' War? (p. 319)

7.   How did the Golden Bull weaken the centralized authority of the Holy Roman Emperor? (p. 320)

8.   What was the political system of most of the northern Italian city-states by the beginning of the fifteenth century? (p. 321)

9.   What family ruled in Florence? (p. 321)

10. What was the title of the ruler of the Ottoman Empire, and on what basis did he claim his authority? (p. 323)

11. What role did slaves play in the Ottoman Empire? (p. 323)

12. The threat of what power stimulated the union of Poland and Lithuania? (p. 323)

REVIEW AND ANTICIPATION

1. Review Frederick II's policy toward his German and Italian lands. Given the decentralization in Germany during the fourteenth century, do you think he was right to invest his time in Sicily?

2. On the map in this chapter, locate Bosnia and Serbia. Since this region is now in Moslem hands, bringing religious diversity to the area, would you expect that to cause problems later?

Chapter 24
Transition in Religion and Thought, 1300-1500

OVERVIEW

The medieval religious forms established in the thirteenth century were confronted with many challenges in the fourteenth, and the Church's response was not entirely effective.

1. <u>The Crisis in Religious Leadership.</u> Newly strengthened monarchs were able to reassert some authority over religious matters and weaken the power of the popes. The papal court abandoned Rome and moved to Avignon, under the influence of the French king. Adding to the crisis was a period when there were two popes elected and competing for control of Christendom. This was resolved by conciliarism, which argued for power to reside in a council of churchmen. This movement failed to reform the church ills; the popes remained powerful in Rome and involved in secular activities, while corruption continued throughout the church hierarchy.

2. <u>Spiritual Disquiet.</u> While the church hierarchy was emphasizing organization and ritual, many believers were looking for other avenues of religious expression. There was a rise in mysticism, in which individuals attempted to experience God directly without the mediation of church structures. Some people attacked church structure directly, arguing that sacraments and priests were not necessary for people's salvation. All this discontent emphasized the fact that the Church was unable to meet the needs of its followers.

3. <u>Intellectual Ferment and Religious Values.</u> The medieval philosophic system established by the scholastics came under attack in the fourteenth century. Franciscan scholars sought to restore the freedom of God (to act illogically) by claiming that God could not be understood through logic. Therefore, they stressed that religious truths should be sought through faith, and logic should focus on the material world. This paved the way for scientific inquiry.

4. <u>New Forces and the Religious Establishment.</u> Forces outside the Church also weakened the medieval religious establishment. Newly strengthened monarchies wanted to develop national churches rather than one international church. The new wealthy capitalist urban classes found the old religious values incompatible with their way of life. New ways of thinking, humanism, increasingly focused on the role of humans in this world, rather than the Church's promise of reward in the next life.

STUDY QUESTIONS

1. What was the "Babylonian Captivity" of the papacy? What activities did these popes stress? What generated the most criticism of these popes?

2. What was the "Great Schism?" How was it resolved? Why did this reduce the prestige of the papacy?

3. In what ways did church corruption permeate the hierarchy below the papacy?

4. What is mysticism? What were some influential individual mystics and groups? How did the philosophical position of Ockham justify mysticism? Why can this religious impulse be threatening to established church hierarchy?

5. On what basis did Wycliffe and Huss criticize the Church? What reforms would they have required of the Church? Do you think the Church could have satisfied them and still remained as strong as it had been in the past? What happened to Wycliffe and Huss?

6. Aside from these organized movements, what other evidence is there of religious ferment in the fourteenth and fifteenth centuries? Which do you think would have the most impact in breaking down the authority of the medieval church?

7. The medieval church had been bolstered by the scholastic thinking of Thomas Aquinas and others. On what basis did Scotus and Ockham challenge this synthesis? How did their approach stimulate explorations that would lead to modern science?

8. What were the three new forces external to the Church that were challenging the authority of the medieval church? Which do you think ultimately will be the most devastating to the old order?

IDENTIFICATION

TRY TO USE EACH OF THESE TERMS AT LEAST ONCE IN ANSWERING THE STUDY QUESTIONS

*Babylonian Captivity	nominalist	*Great Schism
devotio moderna	*Boniface VIII	mystics
*John Wycliffe	*Unam Sanctam*	Thomas à Kempis
flagellants	William of Ockham	Lollards

John Duns Scotus	*conciliar movement	John Huss
humanism	Catherine of Siena	Marsiglio of Padua
Beguines		

CHRONOLOGY

List in chronological order the words in the Identification section that have an asterisk (*). As you list these items, put a circle around those that are contemporary.

SAMPLE QUESTIONS

1.   Over what two issues did Pope Boniface VIII clash with the kings of France and England? (p. 327)

2.   During most of the fourteenth century, where did the popes hold their court and why did many Christians object to that? (p. 328)

3.   What was the Great Schism? (p. 328)

4.   In general, what was the way of life of communal movements that grew up outside the established religious system? (p. 332)

5.   On what basis did Marsiglio of Padua argue that the state should have greater authority than the Church? (p. 333)

6.   What part of Wycliffe's religious thought made him advocate translating the Bible from Latin to English? (p. 333)

7.   Why did John Duns Scotus say that theology was not a proper matter for rational speculation? (pp. 334-335)

8.   Since Ockham rejected the principle that one could reach God by logic, how did he say one could know religious truths? (p. 335)

REVIEW AND ANTICIPATION

1.   Review the reform movements taken on by the papacy in the eleventh and twelfth centuries. Compare and contrast the actions taken by the popes at Avignon with those taken by earlier popes.

2.   The "Retrospect" reviews many of the structures that developed in the Middle Ages that remained central to western European society. Review

these structures. Which do you think is the most important and enduring? Which might still change?

3. Even though the Church banned the ideas of Wycliffe and Huss that challenged its authority, do you expect these ideas to disappear?

Chapter 25
The Renaissance: Italy

OVERVIEW

This chapter discusses the cultural flowering in Italy that began in the fourteenth century that we call the Italian Renaissance. It looks at the origins, characteristics, great accomplishments and decline of this movement.

1. Italian Origins. Fourteenth-century Italy had a number of features that caused the new culture of the Renaissance to develop there. Society was more urban than the north, with economic prosperity and an urban elite that supported and cultivated the arts. Geographically, Italy also benefited from proximity to the East with its advanced commerce and culture.

2. General Nature. General characteristics of the Renaissance include a revival of classical civilization, a praise of secular life, a growth of individualism, and a broadening of education. However, these values were not shared by the whole society. Poor wage earners, small merchants, country people, and most women did not participate in this new learning.

3. Humanism. Humanism emphasizes classical learning and optimistically focuses on human beings and their potential for great accomplishments. Humanism is expressed in literature, the study of classical manuscripts, educational reform and philosophy, and was forwarded by many famous thinkers.

4. Fine Arts. Renaissance characteristics are visibly and vividly portrayed in painting, sculpture, architecture, and music of the fourteenth through the sixteenth centuries. Like the humanist writers, famous artists are still remembered for their works.

5. Decline. During the sixteenth century, the vigor of the Italian Renaissance waned. Along with a shifting of commercial activity north, and Italian political instability, centers of culture also shifted to northern Europe.

MAP EXERCISE

1. Where are the main cities of Renaissance Italy: Florence, Venice, Pisa, and Milan? Where is Tuscany? What is the main city in Tuscany?

2. What separates the Renaissance cities from southern Italy? What isolates them from northern Europe? What do you think are the strengths and weaknesses of this location?

MAP 27.3 Italy, 1454

STUDY QUESTIONS

1.   What were some of the reasons that the new culture of the Renaissance started in Italy? Why would the presence of a lot of commerce and industry (highly practical) lead to growth of the arts?

2.   What were the main characteristics of Renaissance culture? How might these characteristics have grown out of the situation in Italy that you discussed in question #1?

3.   What does the phrase "Renaissance culture was secular" mean? What was the relationship between Renaissance thought and established religion? Include in your discussion the artists that used religious themes as well as the writers and thinkers.

4.   Discuss the status of women in Renaissance culture, and give the names and accomplishments of some famous Renaissance women.

5.   What is the definition of humanism (both the narrow and the broad meaning)? Discuss famous Renaissance people and tell how their accomplishments reflect humanist ideals.

6.   What was the goal of a humanist education? To what degree do we still have those educational goals?

7.   Give evidence for the importance of classical learning to the Renaissance. Include literature, philosophy and the arts in your discussion.

8.   What characteristics does Machiavelli believe a prince should have? How applicable do you think his political philosophy is to today's politics?

9.   What are some characteristics of Renaissance architecture? How do these characteristics express humanist ideals? What are two of the greatest monuments to Renaissance architecture, and who were some of the greatest architects?

10. What were some of the reasons for the decline of Italy as a vigorous cultural center?

IDENTIFICATION

TRY TO USE EACH OF THESE TERMS AT LEAST ONCE IN ANSWERING
THE STUDY QUESTIONS AND MAP EXERCISES

Boccaccio	Alberti	Machiavelli
Leonardo da Vinci	Vittoria Colonna	Christine de Pisan
Properzia Rossi	Dante Alighieri	*Divine Comedy*
vernacular	Brunelleschi	Michelangelo
Decameron	Masaccio	P. della Mirandola
Lorenzo Valla	Marsilio Ficino	Palestrina
Platonic Academy	Titian	Boticelli
Giotto	*The Prince*	Manuel Chrysoloras
Raphael	Petrarch	
St. Peter's		

SAMPLE QUESTIONS

1. What was the name of the popular book written by Castiglione that expresses the versatility that was praised in the Renaissance? (p. 342)

2. To what social groups was the Renaissance limited? (p. 342)

3. What was the name of the text upon which the papacy had based its claim to temporal power, and which was shown to be a forgery by humanist scholars? (p. 344)

4. In what ways did Giotto break from the medieval artistic conventions? (p. 345)

5. What painting technique did Masaccio introduce that has become one of the hallmarks of Renaissance painting? (p. 345)

6. How do da Vinci's *Virgin of the Rocks* and *The Last Supper* exemplify Renaissance humanist ideals? (p. 345)

7. Who painted the ceiling frescoes in the Vatican Sistine Chapel? (p. 346)

8. Who was the greatest Renaissance sculptor, who also designed the dome of St. Peter's cathedral? (p. 350)

9. What musical instruments came into existence during the Renaissance? (p. 350)

10. What musical innovations besides new instruments were developed during the Renaissance? (p. 350)

REVIEW AND ANTICIPATION

1. What specific characteristics of medieval life and thought did Italian Renaissance culture reject?

2. The Italian Renaissance was strongly influenced by the Roman past that was such a direct inheritance of the Italians. How do you think Renaissance and humanist ideals will change when they move north? Do you think they may have different emphases?

3. Italy was always more urban than northern Europe. How do you think that fact will cause Renaissance ideas to change as they move north?

Chapter 26
The Renaissance: The North

OVERVIEW

This chapter describes the impact of humanist ideas as they spread north from Italy. It discusses the ways in which different aspects of humanism were emphasized as the ideas moved from Italy, and describes the famous thinkers who profoundly influenced future generations.

1.   Northern Humanism. Humanist ideas spread from Italy and were applied particularly to religious ideas by great thinkers from Germany, England, and the Netherlands. These writers created works that profoundly affected many areas of society. University curricula began to be changed to broaden the offerings to stress classical learning and introduce humanistic studies. Even more significant, thinkers brought humanist techniques to the study of religion and began to criticize and attempt to reform the traditional church.

2.   Literature. In addition to affecting theologians and philosophers, humanist ideas influenced writers of novels and drama, yielding a great flowering of literary production that explored the individual and his or her role in the world. These great works by people like Shakespeare, Rabelais, Montaigne and others remain classics.

3.   Printing with Movable Type. The spread of humanist ideas was stimulated by the development of printing with movable type and the increased availability of paper (instead of parchment) upon which to print. Thus, ideas could spread more rapidly and to people who previously had little access to written material.

4.   Art, Architecture, and Music. Northern Renaissance art shared many of the characteristics of Italian art, but, just as with the ideas, they were less secular in their expression. The most famous painters were Flemish and German, and the music capital of the north was the Netherlands. Northern Renaissance architecture was less prominent than in Italy, but may be seen in some structures.

5.   Significance of the Renaissance in History. The Renaissance was an influential movement that established themes that will dominate the early modern period.

STUDY QUESTIONS

1.   What specific changes in religious attitudes were advocated by Thomas More and Desiderius Erasmus? Describe one of each of these thinkers' books and the ideas in them.

2.   The chief interests of the famous writers of novels and drama in the north were "... contemporary human beings and the exciting, rapidly expanding material world around them." Discuss how the major works of Shakespeare, Rabelais, and Cervantes confront these issues. Why do you suppose these works are still so popular today?

3.   Some of the northern humanists (particularly in literature) were critical of religion. Which ones, and what was the nature of their criticism?

4.   What technical developments facilitated the spread of the new humanist ideas and writings? What social groups would gain increased access to written material because of these innovations?

5.   In Belgium significant contributions to Renaissance culture were made. Who were their main representatives? In what fields did they make the most impact? Why do you think this area might have served as such a fertile land for the arts?

IDENTIFICATION

TRY TO USE EACH OF THESE TERMS AT LEAST ONCE IN ANSWERING THE STUDY QUESTIONS

Elizabeth I	Desiderius Erasmus	Sir Thomas More
Shakespeare	Edmund Spenser	*Praise of Folly*
Cervantes	François Rabelais	Michel de Montaigne
Johannes Gutenberg	Lope de Vega	*Don Quixote*
Jan Van Eyck	Hubert Van Eyck	*Adoration of the*
Hans Holbein	Albert Dürer	*Mystic Lamb*

SAMPLE QUESTIONS

1.   The Italian Renaissance movement was located primarily in commercial centers. What were the centers of the northern Renaissance movement? (p. 353)

2.   Under whose rule did the Renaissance flower in England? (p. 354)

3.   Who was influential in the development of modern rationalism by his *Essays,* a new literary form that reveals the importance of the individual in Renaissance thought? (p. 355)

4.   How did Shakespeare exemplify the spirit of the Renaissance? (p. 355)

5.   What does "national vernacular" mean? (p. 356)

6.   What was the earliest known book to be printed? (p. 357)

7.   From where did western Europeans learn about printing from carved wooden blocks and about making paper? (p. 356)

8.   What is the main difference in subject matter between the paintings from the Italian and northern renaissances? (p. 357)

9.   What Flemish painters made a significant contribution to developing oil painting? (pp. 357-358)

10.   What German painter made his greatest contribution in portrait painting, painting portraits of Erasmus, Henry VIII, and Sir Thomas More? (p. 358)

11.   What is the largest Renaissance structure outside Italy? (p. 358)

REVIEW AND ANTICIPATION

1.   Think about the characteristics of the Italian Renaissance, and tell how those specific characteristics were expressed in the northern Renaissance writers and artists.

2.   What medieval preoccupations do you see as continuing in this northern Renaissance?

3.   Do you think the northern Renaissance involved people from a more varied social background than did the Italian Renaissance?

4.   As the process of printing written matter becomes even cheaper, what kinds of materials other than great literature will be spread? What do you think will be the most influential kind of written materials?

5.   What aspect of the northern Renaissance do you think will have the most profound influence over the next century?

Chapter 27
The Rise of National States

OVERVIEW

This chapter describes the political events of the late fourteenth and fifteenth centuries, showing the centralizing abilities of the western powers, the lack of unification in Italy and the German states, and the tensions and wars that arose during these transitions.

1. Spain. In the fifteenth century, Spain emerged as a powerful national state. King Ferdinand and Queen Isabella consolidated their power by allying with the lesser nobility and middle class against the powerful nobility. After their long crusade to reconquer the peninsula from Moslems, the rulers pursued a policy to unify their country religiously. They did this at great economic and intellectual cost by persecuting and expelling Jews and Moslems.

2. France. France was also centralized in the fourteenth century under the rule of a king that also supported the middle class at the expense of the traditional nobility. Louis XI completed the consolidation of the French state by bringing many of the provinces under direct royal control. Furthermore, Louis resisted the attempts of Charles the Bold (of Burgundy) to reestablish a competing powerful state in the east. However, Louis' efforts were expensive and did little to help the lower classes, who remained discontented.

3. England. Henry VII worked to weaken the power of the nobility, who had grown strong during years of civil war (the Wars of the Roses). He restricted their private armies, which had become the basis of their power. Henry gained the support of the middle and lower classes and pursued a frugal economic policy that left England stable and prosperous. He had paved the way for England to be a strong national state.

4. Italy, Germany, and the Holy Roman Empire. The regions of Italy and Germany were unable to follow western Europe in forming centralized national states. In spite of the strong Hapsburg family of the Holy Roman Empire, and the imperial ambitions of Charles V, the forces of decentralization continued throughout the early modern period.

5. International Rivalries, 1516-1559. The centralized state of France and the Holy Roman Emperor fought many wars to try to increase the power of each at the expense of the other. At the same time, a strengthened Ottoman Empire under the Turks threatened Europe in the east.

MAP EXERCISE

See map on p. 122.

1.   Locate Paris, Rome, London, Naples, Florence, Genoa, Vienna, Berlin, Constantinople, Moscow, Warsaw. What is it about the location of these cities that makes them so continually important in European history?

2.   Shade the Hapsburg lands inherited by Charles V. What country would have felt most threatened by these extensive holdings? Mark the territories that were under dispute in the international rivalries of the early sixteenth century between Charles and France.

3.   Shade the Ottoman Empire. Now show where Vienna is. Can you see why the siege of Vienna was significant in stopping the Ottoman advance into Europe?

STUDY QUESTIONS

1.   In consolidating their rule over their national states, the fifteenth-century rulers of Spain, France and England supported the same social group as a way of keeping power. What social group was that? What measures did they institute to support that group? Is the power base of our modern nations the same social group that gained royal support in the fifteenth century?

2.   What are laws against livery and maintenance? What was their purpose and why do you think they would have been effective in achieving their purpose?

3.   What was the form of government in the following Italian states: Florence, Venice, Milan, Naples? What was the main source of wealth of Florence, Venice, and Milan?

4.   What were the forces that kept the German emperors from unifying the German-speaking peoples? Why was the Diet ineffective as a unifying force of Germany?

5.   Charles V inherited vast lands in Europe, and fought a number of wars to increase his holdings. With whom did he fight most of these wars? What was the result? What did Charles finally do with the lands he inherited?

6.   Centralizing monarchies were intended to end feudal warfare and bring peace. They did not bring peace; they just changed the nature of the wars. How?

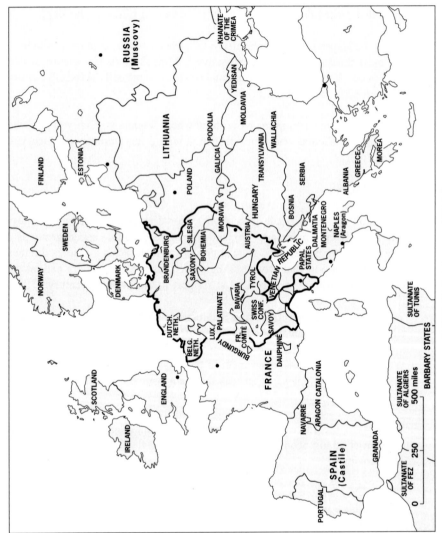

MAP 27.2 Europe, 1526

IDENTIFICATION

TRY TO USE EACH OF THESE TERMS AT LEAST ONCE IN ANSWERING
THE STUDY QUESTIONS AND MAP EXERCISES

*Ferdinand and Isabella	Marranos	Moriscos
*Henry VII	*Louis XI	*Charles the Bold
*Charles V	livery	*Treaty of Lodi
*Suleiman	Hapsburg	bourgeoisie
Valois	*Treaty of Cateau-Cambrésis	*Philip II

CHRONOLOGY

List in chronological order the words in the Identification section that have an asterisk
(*). As you list these items, put a circle around those that are contemporary.

SAMPLE QUESTIONS

1.   The coins, commonly called the "dollar" were widely circulated from the
      sixteenth to the eighteenth centuries. From what country were these coins?
      (p. 363)

2.   Why did the Catholic sovereigns of Spain exile the Jews from their country?
      (p. 362)

3.   Which social class benefited least by the consolidation of France achieved by
      Louis XI? (p. 363)

4.   What is the name of the successful early modern dynasty established in
      England by Henry VII? (p. 363)

5.   What was the main reason for Italian disunity in the early modern period?
      (p. 366)

6.   How were the Holy Roman Emperors chosen? (p. 366)

7.   What was Charles V's most significant military accomplishment? (p. 369)

8.   What religion was practiced by the Ottoman Turks? (p. 369)

9.   Who became the king of Spain after Charles V? (p. 369)

10.   What was the result of the Treaty of Cateau-Cambrésis? (p. 369)

11.   What was the name of the dynasty of France under Francis I that fought in the dynastic wars against the Hapsburgs? (p. 369)

REVIEW AND ANTICIPATION

1.   Who were the antagonists in the Hundred Years' War and the Wars of the Roses? Why do you think these wars would have made it hard for Henry VII to break the power of the nobility?

2.   Who were the Ottoman Turks? When did they first appear in Europe? What was the strength of their political system?

3.   Which areas of Europe at the end of the sixteenth century do you think will prove to be the most politically unstable?

4.   What do you think will be the long-term result of the Turkish presence in the Balkan areas of eastern Europe?

Chapter 28
European Expansion, Commercial Capitalism, and Social Change

OVERVIEW

This chapter describes the expansion of European civilization to many parts of the world, and details the economic and social changes that supported and grew from this expansion.

1. The Age of Discovery. In the late fifteenth and early sixteenth centuries, European explorers were highly motivated to explore beyond the boundaries of Europe. The Portuguese and Spanish were in the forefront of the explorations, and ended up circumnavigating the globe and opening the New World for settlement and exploitation.

2. The Founding of the Spanish New World Empire. Spanish explorers encountered a number of highly organized, advanced native tribes in the New World. Although these peoples had well developed social structures and religion, and many artistic accomplishments, their technological level was not able to withstand European conquest. Their civilizations were almost wholly destroyed and replaced by an imposed Christian-Spanish culture.

3. Capitalism and the Commercial Revolution. The new discoveries fueled a growth in commerce that was so dramatic it is known as the "commercial revolution." This revolution included the growth of a capitalist system with related structures, like banking, chartered companies, joint stock companies, commercialization of agriculture, and a "putting out" system. The Italian city-states were the first to prosper from this new revolution, but soon the center moved north to the Hanseatic League, Amsterdam and London.

4. Mercantilism. Governments desiring to profit from the new commercial revolution developed an economic theory that advocated government regulation of the economy to seek a favorable balance of trade for governments to acquire gold and silver.

5. Political and Social Consequences. Some groups gained and some lost in the economic upheavals of the commercial revolution. Absolute monarchs, the middle class, landlords, and wealthier peasants who adapted to the new agriculture benefited, providing new social mobility for some people. Old nobility, urban poor, and many peasants became more poor, with increased misery. Women's economic status was probably reduced with commercial capitalism.

6.   <u>European Domination of the Globe.</u> The commercial revolution and the dramatic explorations it supported led to the spread of European civilization all over the world. This spread had a varied impact in various parts of the world, virtually destroying some civilizations and simply influencing others. But from the sixteenth century through the nineteenth, the spread of European civilization was a profoundly influential movement in world history.

MAP EXERCISE

1.   Which of the shaded areas was claimed by Portugal and which by Spain? What treaty determined this division?

2.   Where are the Pacific, Atlantic, and Indian oceans? Where are the Straits of Magellan? What ocean was made accessible by the successful negotiation of these Straits? Where is the Cape of Good Hope? What was made accessible by the successful rounding of this Cape?

STUDY QUESTIONS

1.   What were the motivations of the explorers? Be sure to consider all their motives, not just the ones that might most motivate us in the twentieth century.

2.   What countries were first in the explorations? Who were the main explorers and where did they go?

3.   What were the main tribes of the indigenous peoples that the Spaniards and Portuguese encountered in the New World? What were the main organizational structures and accomplishments of these tribes? Was their social structure more egalitarian than that of the Europeans?

4.   Look at the portrayals of the encounter between Europeans and native Americans in Figures 28.1 and 28.2. How did the Europeans view the natives? What features of the Europeans did the Aztecs emphasize? Do any elements of these portrayals continue in our views today?

5.   What are the main elements of capitalism? What business organizations were developed to forward this capitalist enterprise?

6.   How was the growth of commerce related to the growth of slave trade?

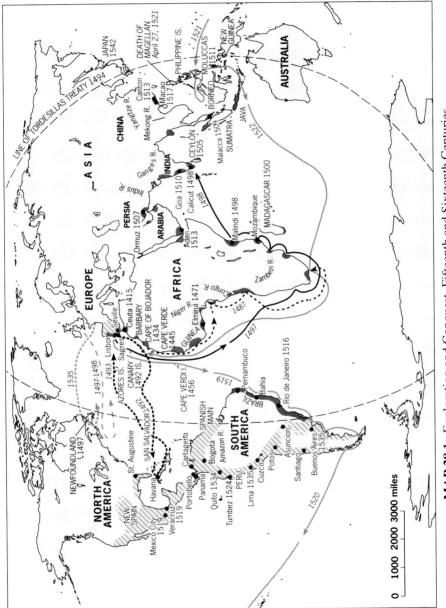

MAP 28.1 Exploration and Conquest, Fifteenth and Sixteenth Centuries

7.   What were the main centers of the commercial revolution? Which were the earliest and which were later? Why didn't Spain and Portugal enter the new commerce as quickly as other regions?

8.   What is mercantilism? What policies would a government pursue in support of mercantilist aims? How is mercantilism related to countries' desire to hold colonies?

9.   What social groups lost and which gained in the new commercial revolution? Why? Which social groups are most vulnerable today to rapid economic change?

IDENTIFICATION

TRY TO USE EACH OF THESE TERMS AT LEAST ONCE IN ANSWERING THE STUDY QUESTIONS AND MAP EXERCISES

Henry the Navigator	Prester John	Vasco da Gama
Cabral	C. Columbus	Joint Stock Company
Ponce de León	de Soto	Treaty of Tordesillas
Magellan	Balboa	Coronado
Cortez	Pizarro	John Cabot
Jacques Cartier	Aztec	Inca
Maya	ideographs	Toltec
capitalism	Jacob Fugger	
mercantilism		

SAMPLE QUESTIONS

1.   What goods did the Portuguese bring from West Africa? (p. 371)

2.   Where did Columbus think he had arrived when he reached the West Indies? (p. 371)

3.   Where did the English and French go in their explorations? (p. 373)

4.   What were the two most highly organized native societies the Spanish encountered in the New World? (p. 373)

5.   From where did the first inhabitants of the Western Hemisphere originally come? (p. 373)

6.   What tribe centered its empire where modern Mexico City is? (p. 373)

7. Which native tribe developed a highly sophisticated system of mathematics and an advanced calendar? (p. 373)

8. Give a simple definition of capitalism. (p. 375)

9. What new goods fueled the commercial revolution? (p. 375)

10. Where was the Hanseatic League centered? (p. 375)

11. What things contributed to the inflation of the sixteenth century? (p. 377)

12. What is the basic assumption of mercantilist theory? (p. 378)

13. What social group was hardest hit by inflation? (p. 379)

REVIEW AND ANTICIPATION

1. Which of the Renaissance characteristics that you studied before might have contributed to the increased interest in discovering previously unknown areas of the world?

2. Why do you think the Italian city-states were in the forefront of the commercial revolution?

3. In the last chapter, we saw many absolute monarchs allying with the middle class to help strengthen their power. Why was that a particularly good idea given what you have learned in this chapter? In what countries did monarchs ally with nobility instead? Was that a good idea?

3. What group do you think will attempt to overturn the economic controls that are basic to mercantilist theory?

Chapter 29
The Reformation

OVERVIEW

In the sixteenth century, the Christian unity of western Europe was divided into various competing Christian denominations. These splits involved political, economic, and social upheavals and profoundly transformed European society.

1. Background. In the fourteenth and fifteenth centuries, the traditional Church had been plagued by crises and complaints. In the sixteenth century, further criticism was added due to changes especially in the region of the Holy Roman Empire. These changes led to forces of protest that could not be suppressed.

2. Lutheranism. Martin Luther, a German monk, initiated the first successful reform movement against the Catholic church. Luther emphasized piety and faith over dogma and ritual, and reacted against doctrinal abuses like the selling of indulgences. The theological revolt was helped by political instability in the German regions: Peasants revolted, princes and cities wanted independence and the emperor was involved in foreign wars. The Peace of Augsburg allowed Lutheranism as a religious option.

3. Calvinism. John Calvin was influenced by Luther and further developed Protestant theology. He focused on the majesty of God and predestination, and established a reformed city in Geneva, Switzerland, where the principles of Calvinism were enforced. Late in the sixteenth century, Calvinism replaced Lutheranism as the dominant force of Protestantism.

4. Anglicanism. Henry VIII, king of England, broke away from the Catholic church and declared himself head of the Church of England in order to divorce his wife. This began the process of moving England to Protestantism that was completed under his daughter Elizabeth I.

5. The Anabaptists. Some sects arose that believed the other reformers did not go far enough. These "radical" Protestants in general appealed to the poor and rejected allegiance with civil government. They believed in a church of Christians that were "born again" into the Holy Spirit, and they were persecuted by Catholics and other Protestants alike.

6. Catholic Reform. The Catholic church addressed the challenge of Protestantism by meeting in the Council of Trent to eliminate abuses and confirm its traditional doctrines. The Society of Jesus with its emphasis on

obedience, education, and missionary work was a powerful force in revitalizing the Catholic church.

7.   Women and the Reformation. The Protestant movement encouraged companionate marriages and the acceptance of sexuality, but it did not appreciably provide for women to serve in any leadership roles. The Catholic reform movement did not improve the status of average women, but it did provide for women to express their spirituality actively and influentially in convents, an option foreclosed by Protestants.

8.   Summary. Political and economic factors served to forward the implementation of Protestantism. While the Protestant sects differed among each other, they shared a number of characteristics. Western Christendom was split between the hostile camps of Protestantism and reformed Catholicism.

STUDY QUESTIONS

1.   What were some of the general complaints about the traditional Church that led to the Protestant reformation?

2.   What were the main religious principles Luther introduced? What was his position on sacraments, salvation, monasteries, and clerical celibacy? How did these views arise from abuses he observed?

3.   What groups benefited most from the religious reformation proposed by Luther? How was Lutheranism ultimately adopted? In what countries did it receive the greatest support?

4.   What were the main religious principles advocated by John Calvin? How were his ideas similar to Luther's and how were they different?

5.   Describe the Calvinist society established in Geneva. Be sure to discuss social and cultural patterns, as well as the system of church government he introduced. In what countries was Calvinism most popular?

6.   How did Protestantism arrive in England? What was the difference in religious policy between Henry VIII and Elizabeth I? What was Elizabeth's "compromise settlement"? Which groups remained dissatisfied with this compromise?

7.   What were the characteristics of "radical" sects like Anabaptist? To what social class did these groups most appeal? Give some examples of these sects

and their leaders. Are there religions of this sort today? What do you think contributes to their modern popularity?

8.   Catholic reformers as early as the early sixteenth century discussed ways the Church should be reformed. What were some of these early reform inclinations? What were the two main schools of thought about how Catholicism should confront the Protestant challenge? Which one won?

9.   What were the main findings of the Council of Trent? How do you think these decisions virtually assured that there would be no reconciliation between Catholics and Protestants?

10.   How was the Society of Jesus influential in the newly reformed Catholicism?

11.   What benefits did Protestantism offer women? What benefits did Catholicism offer women? What evidence is there that the fifteenth and sixteenth centuries were a repressive time for women?

12.   The Protestant Reformation involved a number of complex political, economic, cultural, and religious issues. What are some of the interpretations about the meaning of the Reformation? Which do you think is most convincing? Why?

IDENTIFICATION

TRY TO USE EACH OF THESE TERMS AT LEAST ONCE IN ANSWERING THE STUDY QUESTIONS

Erasmus	John Wycliffe	Thomas Müntzer
John Huss	John Tetzel	Anabaptist
indulgence	Peace of Augsburg	Edward VI
John Calvin	Society of Friends	Martin Luther
predestination	Fifth Lateran Council	Jesuits
Henry VIII	Index of Forbidden	Mennonites
Elizabeth I	Books	Ignatius Loyola
Cardinal Contarini	Ninety-Five Theses	Act of Supremacy
Council of Trent	transubstantiation	Cardinal Ximenes
simony	Charles V	Francis Xavier
Society of Jesus	John Knox	Quakers
Ursulines	Teresa of Avila	Huldreich Zwingli

SAMPLE QUESTIONS

1. Which of the four major Protestant movements was chronologically the earliest? (p. 383)

2. What did Martin Luther believe was the true means of salvation? (p. 383)

3. What sacraments did Martin Luther keep? (p. 385)

4. In what city did John Calvin establish a model Protestant state? (p. 386)

5. What Protestant denomination particularly dignified hard work? (p. 386)

6. Who took the title "Defender of the Faith?" (p. 387)

7. The Council of Trent's decisions were in two categories: dogmatic and reformatory. Give an example of each type of decision. (p. 389)

8. What mechanisms did the Catholic church establish to enforce the decrees of the Council of Trent? (p. 389)

9. What was the guiding principle required of all members of the Jesuit order that helped make it such a powerful force for the reformed Catholicism? (p. 389)

10. What characteristics did all Protestant sects share? (p. 393)

REVIEW AND ANTICIPATION

1. Review the crises in the fourteenth century Church that formed the background for some of the criticism that was brought by the reformers.

2. What characteristics of the Renaissance do you think are expressed by these Protestant reformers?

3. How well do you think people of these different religious beliefs will get along? Do you think the belief that people should choose their religious beliefs will lead to greater religious toleration?

Chapter 30
Politics and the Wars of Religion

OVERVIEW

The religious struggles of the Protestant Reformation came to the political front in the sixteenth century, introducing a period of violent religious warfare.

1.   The Crusade of Catholic Spain. Philip II, king of Spain, the Netherlands, Milan, Naples and Sardinia was a rich and powerful Catholic king who attempted to restore lands lost to Protestantism. He fought wars in the Netherlands, which ultimately led to the division of the Netherlands into a Catholic south and Protestant north. He also attempted to restore Catholicism to England by marrying Queen Mary. After Mary's death, he tried to conquer England with his navy, but he failed. His greatest success was diminishing the Turkish menace in the Mediterranean.

2.   The Religious Wars in France. In the sixteenth century there were struggles in France between Catholics and Protestants, especially French Calvinists called "Huguenots." These disputes led to massacres in the name of religion. Peace was finally restored by the accession to the throne of Henry IV who supported religious toleration.

3.   The Thirty Years' War in Germany. Unresolved religious issues combined with political and dynastic struggles to erupt into a destructive war that ravaged German lands. Protestant Scandinavian kings, German princes and French nobility fought against Catholic princes and Hapsburgs. After devastating Germany, the war ended, ending the religious warfare that had dominated the century.

MAP EXERCISE

1.   Highlight the areas on the map that were ruled by Philip II. Which of those areas was predominantly Protestant? Which country will be divided along religious lines after the wars of Philip II?

2.   Where is the Holy Roman Empire? Where is Austria, Norway, Sweden? Why do you think the Scandinavian countries and Austria were so interested in getting involved in the Thirty Years' War?

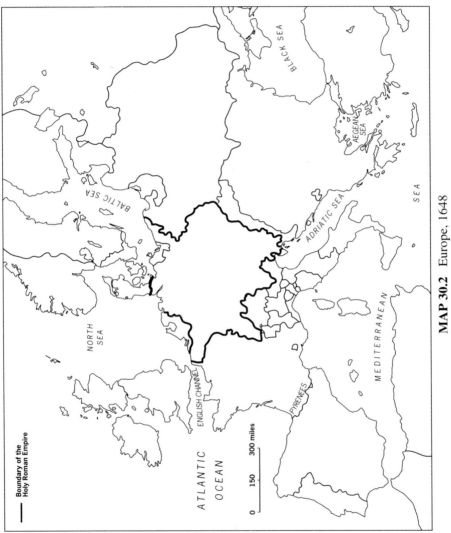

MAP 30.2 Europe, 1648

Boundary of the
Holy Roman Empire

BLACK SEA

BALTIC SEA

AEGEAN
SEA

ADRIATIC SEA

SEA

NORTH
SEA

MEDITERRANEAN

ENGLISH CHANNEL

PYRENEES

ATLANTIC
OCEAN

0   150   300 miles

STUDY QUESTIONS

1. In what regions did Philip II's strong commitment to Catholicism lead to warfare? Did he succeed in imposing Catholicism by warfare? What regions were driven more firmly to Protestantism?

2. What sequence of events led to the division of the Netherlands? What were the main issues leading to the division? What two countries resulted from the division?

3. What sequence of events in France led to an ultimate religious compromise in that country? What was the compromise? What king established this compromise?

4. Who were the opponents in the Thirty Years' War? What were the issues of the war? What were the results of the war (include political, religious, and social effects)?

IDENTIFICATION

TRY TO USE EACH OF THESE TERMS AT LEAST ONCE IN ANSWERING THE STUDY QUESTIONS AND MAP EXERCISES

Philip II	William of Orange	Union of Utrecht
politique	Spanish Armada	Elizabeth I
Battle of Lepanto	Suleiman	Don Juan
Huguenots	Hapsburgs	Henry of Navarre
Edict of Nantes	Gustavus Adolphus	Peace of Augsburg
Bourbons	Christian IV	Albrecht von
Peace of Westphalia		Wallenstein

SAMPLE QUESTIONS

1. What religion dominates in the Dutch Netherlands? (p. 396)

2. What was the principal motivation for Philip II's marriage to Mary Tudor? (p. 398)

3. What small republic led the world in commerce, banking, painting, science, and philosophy in the seventeenth century? (pp. 397-398)

4. Why did the Spanish Armada sail against England? (p. 398)

5. What event greatly diminished the Turkish menace to Christendom by sea? (p. 399)

6. What Protestant sect made the most impact in France? (p. 400)

7. What powerful family supported the Catholic cause in France? (p. 400)

8. What powerful family initially supported the Protestant cause in France, who later became rulers? (p. 400)

9. What was the St. Bartholomew's Day massacre? (p. 400)

10. What religion did King Henry IV of France take in order to bring peace to his country? (p. 400)

11. What Protestant group was left out of the Peace of Augsburg settlement? (p. 400)

12. Who were the Protestant leaders in the Thirty Years' War? (pp. 401-402)

13. Who was the famous Catholic general in the Thirty Years' War? (p. 402)

14. What treaty recognized the independence of Switzerland and the Dutch Netherlands? (p. 402)

REVIEW AND ANTICIPATION

1. Review the Peace of Augsburg. What was the compromise? Why did it fall apart in the sixteenth century?

2. Review Elizabeth I's religious position. How do you think her approach to religious issues might have been influenced by Philip II's policies?

3. The Thirty Years' War left Germany even more divided than it had been before. Do you think that will lead to instability in this region?

Chapter 31
Society, Faith, and Culture in the
Seventeenth and Eighteenth Centuries

OVERVIEW

The society and culture of the seventeenth and eighteenth centuries were dominated by the tastes and courts of absolute monarchs. Profoundly influential literature and art movements emerged under their patronage while social patterns were changing.

1. Society. This section describes the social and economic base of seventeenth- and eighteenth-century society. Population declines and growths provided the background for changes in the social structure that remained resistant to much social mobility. Most people continued to live on the land in small villages, although changes in agriculture and patterns of production began to change traditional rural ways of life. An "agricultural revolution" that improved existing products and developed new methods helped increase yields. To increase agricultural efficiency, old common fields were enclosed. Peasants increasingly supplemented their income by "cottage industry." Cities grew, bringing new opportunities for some and new poverty for others. Even the basic institution of society, the family, underwent changes during the eighteenth century, leading to family life that is more close to our own. Women were considered subordinate to men, and the roles of women varied depending upon their social class.

2. Faith: The Growth of Pietism. New religious sects grew that stressed faith and social activism through private charity. These influential movements were not revolutionary, but they emphasized working within the political status quo to effect social improvements. Therefore, they were able to make a significant impact on their societies.

3. Culture. The seventeenth and eighteenth centuries were marked by cultural advances in literature, painting, architecture and music. Most of these styles (baroque, classical, and rococo) reflected and perpetuated aristocratic tastes. However, in the Dutch Netherlands and England the increasingly wealthy middle class began to make their presence felt as patrons of the arts. The lower classes also had cultural outlets that were different from those that had developed in the courts of absolute rulers. They participated in festivals with music, dancing, feasts and generally rowdy celebrations. They enjoyed sports that brought communities together. The most popular were animal fights and soccer and cricket. The lines between the cultural tastes of the classes were beginning to blur, as classes mingled at sporting events and lower classes became more literate.

STUDY QUESTIONS

1. What were the population trends in the seventeenth and eighteenth centuries? What are the results of population growth on the lives of people? Do we see many of those same results today?

2. Describe the social structure of society. Include in your discussion of the various social classes 1) where they get their wealth and prestige, 2) what their function in society is, and 3) how easily they might change their status.

3. What social classes are shown in the paintings illustrated in the text? How are these classes portrayed? What stereotypes of the social classes are shown in the paintings?

4. What innovations were so important that their adoption introduced what has been called an "agricultural revolution"?

5. What were the advantages of urban life? What were the disadvantages? Does modern urban life hold these same advantages and disadvantages?

6. Describe the significant changes that occurred in family life during the second half of the eighteenth century. In which class were women most likely to work outside the home? Doing what? Which of these characteristics of family life do you find the most different from modern times?

7. What were the characteristics of eighteenth-century literature? How were these characteristics consistent with the values of absolute monarchs? Give some examples of authors and/or texts to demonstrate your point.

8. In the seventeenth and eighteenth centuries, there were three main styles of visual arts. What were they? What were the main characteristics of each? Give some examples of artists and/or works to demonstrate your point.

9. How did the music of the period also reflect many of these same characteristics? Who were the famous musical composers?

IDENTIFICATION

TRY TO USE EACH OF THESE TERMS AT LEAST ONCE IN ANSWERING THE STUDY QUESTIONS

Poor Laws	Jonathan Swift	El Greco
Quakers	Henry Fielding	Rembrandt van Rijn
Voltaire	baroque	Versailles

rococo	Jethro Tull	G.F. Handel
J.S. Bach	George Fox	St. Peter's
W.A. Mozart	Molière	Gainsborough
Charles Townsend	Saint-Simon	Velásquez
enclosures	John Milton	F.J. Haydn
pietism	*Paradise Lost*	classicism
John Wesley	Peter Paul Rubens	Christopher Wren
Blaise Pascal	Jan Vermeer	*Night Watch*
Rousseau		

SAMPLE QUESTIONS

1.   The aristocracy was the highest social class in the seventeenth and eighteenth centuries. While they were not always rich, from where did they get the money they had? (p. 407)

2.   What country is known for initiating most of the agricultural innovations that led to the agricultural revolution? (p. 408)

3.   Most cottage industry was engaged in producing what? (p. 408)

4.   How did the increasingly wealthy members of the middle class use their wealth to try to rise into the aristocracy? (p. 410)

5.   What careers were open to unmarried middle-class women of the seventeenth and eighteenth centuries? (p. 411)

6.   What were the characteristics of pietistic sects? (p. 412)

7.   Where did paintings and literature often reflect the tastes of the middle class? (p. 413)

8.   What were the major common denominators of the golden age of French literature? (p. 413)

9.   Who wrote the most popular French novel of the period, *Grand Cyrus*, under her brother's name to avoid discrimination? (p. 413)

10.   What literary form was developed in England in the eighteenth century that was aimed at and reflected the tastes of the middle class? (p. 414)

11.   What is the main thing that sets the painting of the Dutch Netherlands apart from that of other countries? (p. 416)

12. What musical instruments developed rapidly in the seventeenth century? (p. 417)

13. What kinds of music did Mozart compose? (p. 418)

REVIEW AND ANTICIPATION

1. You can see the middle class beginning to get rich and participate in cultural activities. What do you think they are going to want to be involved in next? Will the aristocracy be able to hold onto its privileged position?

2. Do you think the arts will continue to reflect aristocratic tastes? Why or why not?

Chapter 32
Royal Absolutism in Western
and Eastern Europe

OVERVIEW

In the seventeenth century, the rulers of some European states were able to exert absolute royal rule as a political system. These states grew strong and shaped the politics of Europe in the early modern period.

1. Absolutism in Western Europe: France. The origins of absolute monarchy in France began in the sixteenth century with the careful policies of Henry IV that weakened the nobility and strengthened the monarchy. Henry helped the state prosper by encouraging new industries and granting religious toleration. These sensible policies were not continued after his death, so the economy of France was weakened. Yet, the strong monarchy did persist to be handed down to Louis XIV in whose extremely capable hands royal absolutism reached its height. Under Louis' reign, the idea of "divine right" monarchy was articulated that offered a theoretical base for absolute government. He moved his court to Versailles and kept the nobility under close control. As a divine right ruler, Louis persecuted religious minorities and engaged in aggressive wars to enhance his power. His expensive wars left a legacy that made his weaker successors unable to sustain the strength of royal power.

2. Absolutism in Eastern Europe. During the seventeenth and eighteenth centuries three states in eastern Europe grew strong and developed absolute monarchies. The Hohenzollern dynasty in Prussia carefully built its power on the basis of a strong military and fiscal responsibility. It was successful enough to be able to extend its territories. The Hapsburg dynasty of Austria was also successful in centralizing its authority and extending its territory. Russia under the Romanovs built its absolutist government at the expense of its neighbors. In addition, the ruling elites further repressed the serfs until they were reduced to almost the status of slaves. These states of Prussia, Austria, and Russia soon dominated the east at the expense of their neighbors, especially Poland, Sweden and the Ottoman Empire.

MAP EXERCISE

1. Highlight the state of Prussia. Where is Berlin? What is the most obvious weakness of this state? What area would be most threatened by its efforts to consolidate its territory?

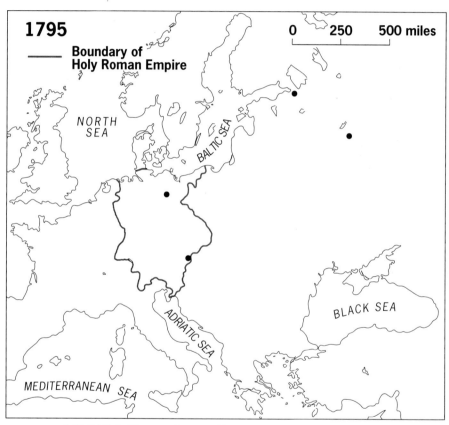

MAP 32.3 Eastern Europe, Sixteenth – Eighteenth Centuries

See map on p. 143.

2.   Where is Austria? Where is Vienna? What states would most readily threaten Austria?

3.   Where is Moscow? Where is St. Petersburg? Why is the location of St. Petersburg consistent with Peter the Great's desire to bring Russia into closer contact with the West?

4.   Locate Poland, Sweden, and the Ottoman Empire. Why were these states vulnerable to their neighbors? Which neighbors took most advantage of them?

STUDY QUESTIONS

1.   What were the actions of Louis XIV's predecessors that allowed him to inherit a strong centralized state with a great deal of royal power? (Include both domestic and foreign activities in your discussion.) What caused the decline of French absolutism?

2.   What is the theory of divine right monarchy? What political philosopher was its main proponent, and under whose reign was it developed? In the reign of Louis XIV was this theory consistent with religious toleration?

3.   What policies did the Hohenzollerns of Prussia use to increase their power? What does the painting in Illustration 32.1 reveal about the things the Prussians emphasized in strengthening their power?

4.   What was the dynasty that ruled in Austria? What were the main policies of the ruler? What were its main problems?

5.   How did Russia grow to prominence until the Romanov rule in the seventeenth century? What did Peter I (the Great) do to increase his own power and the power of the Russian state?

6.   What social changes did Peter the Great introduce as part of his desire to model Russia after the western powers? What social group was affected the least by these changes?

7.   Did the revolt of Pugachev (under Catherine the Great) bring the status of peasants closer to that of western peasants?

8. At the beginning of the eighteenth century, Poland included a large territory. In view of this, why wasn't Poland a strong state? (Include economic, political, and social reasons.)

IDENTIFICATION

TRY TO USE EACH OF THESE TERMS AT LEAST ONCE IN ANSWERING THE STUDY QUESTIONS AND MAP EXERCISES

*Henry IV	Huguenot	*Edict of Nantes
*Marie de Médicis	*Fronde*	*Richelieu
*Mazarin	Versailles	Colbert
Bossuet	Huguenot	mercantilism
Jansenist	Hohenzollern	*Great Elector
*Treaty of Utrecht	*Frederick	*Frederick II
*Frederick I	William I	*Ivan III
*Maria Theresa	Hapsburg	*Michael Romanov
*Ivan IV (Terrible)		

CHRONOLOGY

List in chronological order the words in the Identification section that have an asterisk (*). As you list these items, put a circle around those that are contemporary.

SAMPLE QUESTIONS

1. What new industries did Henry IV encourage in France that helped increase the royal income? (p. 421)

2. Which French ruler believed in religious toleration and increased prosperity for the lower classes? (p. 421)

3. Describe the economic policy that has come to be called Colbertism and give its drawbacks. (p. 423)

4. What was Louis XIV's religious policy, and how did it grow out of the concept of divine right monarchy? (pp. 423-424)

5. What were the terms of the Treaty of Utrecht? (p. 425)

6. What things undermined the power of the French monarchs after Louis XIV? (p. 425)

7. What countries partitioned Poland in the eighteenth century? (p. 427)

8.   What Czar attempted to westernize Russia, and what steps did he take to do so? (pp. 428-429)

9.   What feature of the Polish legislature (the Diet) led to it being almost impossible to pass anything and thus to virtual political anarchy? (p. 430)

10.   In addition to Poland, what two other European states were weakened territorially by the growing strength of Austria, Prussia, and Russia? (p. 431)

11.   Why was Sweden unable to hold its far-flung territories, and which countries took its territories east and south of the Baltic? (p. 431)

REVIEW AND ANTICIPATION

1.   How is the baroque art described in the last chapter consistent with the political philosophy described here?

2.   What social group do you think was hindered by the economic policy of mercantilism? Do you expect a new economic theory to develop that will address their concerns?

3.   Given the increased oppression in the east under the absolute monarchs, what social group do you think will ultimately revolt?

Chapter 33
The Challenge to Absolutism:
England and the Dutch Netherlands

OVERVIEW

This chapter discusses the growth of representative democracy in England and the Dutch Netherlands during a time when absolutism was the dominant political thought elsewhere.

1. Early Stuart Attempts at Absolutism. James I and Charles I attempted to exert absolute authority in England. Their early efforts were frustrated by Parliament. Charles finally thought there were enough divisions within Parliament for him to try by force to become an absolute rather than a limited monarch.

2. Civil War, Commonwealth, and Protectorate, 1642-1660. In 1642 a civil war began between the forces of Parliament and those of the monarchy. Under the leadership of Cromwell, the parliamentary forces won, and replaced the monarchy. Ultimately, Parliament declared a "Protectorate" in which Cromwell was virtually an absolute monarch. Cromwell established religious toleration for Protestants, attempted to subdue rebellious Irish and Scots, and promoted colonial interests. Cromwell's son was unable to continue to rule. Parliament reintroduced the monarchy and placed the son of Charles I on the throne.

3. The Restoration, 1660-1688. During the Restoration (the return of Stuart rule) the old struggles between monarchy and Parliament continued, revealing an ongoing power struggle over who held ultimate authority. The problems were compounded by the Stuarts' support for Catholicism. Circumstances came to a head in 1688 when Parliament invited William and Mary of Orange to take the throne. A "bloodless revolution" had occurred.

4. The Glorious Revolution and Its Consequences. The "Glorious Revolution" was the largely nonviolent establishment of the reign of William and Mary. This change in government marked the victory of Parliament over absolute monarchs and the establishment in Britain of a limited monarchy. As a consequence of this victory, Parliament began to take an increasing role in affairs of state, and the political forms that mark Britain's system took shape.

5. The United Netherlands. When the people of the Netherlands won their freedom from the absolute monarch Philip II, they established a nation with a republican form of government. This government offered many freedoms

(including religious toleration) for its citizens. In this environment, the Dutch became leaders in commerce, art, and science in the seventeenth century.

STUDY QUESTIONS

1. What were the circumstances in England that interfered with the Stuart kings' desire to impose absolute rule? Be sure to consider economic, social, organizational, and religious circumstances.

2. What were Parliament's main objections to James I? What were Parliament's objections to Charles I?

3. Describe the course of the English civil war. Include a discussion of the supporters of both sides, and their aims. Who won? What was the main factor that determined the winning side?

4. What two forms of government were tried in England after the civil war until 1660? Why did each fail?

5. Who was initially brought to the throne by the Restoration? What policies of the Protectorate were overturned by the king? What problems remained? How did the Restoration period end?

6. What was the "Glorious Revolution"? What limits on royal power did Parliament impose?

7. Describe the "cabinet system" that emerged in the eighteenth century. What circumstances made its development necessary?

8. What foreign policy did William of Orange introduce? In what regions were most of his involvements? Are there modern consequences to his policies?

9. Describe the form of government established in the Netherlands. Describe the Dutch leadership role in commerce. Do you think there is a relationship between the politics and economics in this case? Do we associate democracy with free enterprise today?

10. Discuss the accomplishments of the Dutch in the arts and philosophy, and science. Do you think these accomplishments are a result of their economic successes or their political system?

IDENTIFICATION

TRY TO USE EACH OF THESE TERMS AT LEAST ONCE IN ANSWERING THE STUDY QUESTIONS

*James I	*Charles I	Petition of Rights
Star Chamber	*Short Parliament	*Long Parliament
*Oliver Cromwell	Cavalier	Roundheads
*Rump Parliament	*Commonwealth	Levellers
*Restoration	*Charles II	*Protectorate
Tories	Whigs	*James II
*William of Orange	*Glorious Revolution	John Locke
Jan Vermeer	*George I	*George II
Rembrandt van Rijn		

CHRONOLOGY

List in chronological order the words in the Identification section that have an asterisk (*). As you list these items, put a circle around those that are contemporary.

SAMPLE QUESTIONS

1. The House of Commons in England theoretically represented the entire populace, but what groups actually dominated it? (p. 434)

2. What caused the Scots to rebel in 1639 and invade northern England? (p. 435)

3. What social and political programs did the Levellers advocate? (p. 436)

4. Under Cromwell's influence, what position did the Rump Parliament take on the Anglican church, the House of Lords and the monarchy? (p. 437)

5. What happened to Charles I after the civil war? (p. 437)

6. Who was declared the Lord Protector for life of England? (p. 437)

7. The Clarendon Code reestablished the Anglican church, but what groups were left out of the religious toleration? (p. 438)

8. What bill passed in 1689 granted, among other things, freedom of speech to Parliament members and no taxation without representation? (p. 439)

9.   Who wrote the *Two Treatises on Civil Government* that established the political principle of government as a contract? (p. 439)

10.   What is the title of the official who leads the British cabinet and who is the leader of the majority party in the House of Commons? (p. 441)

11.   What treaty established the independence of the United Netherlands? (p. 441)

12.   In what industries did the Dutch grow wealthy and serve all of Europe? (p. 442)

13.   What inventions did the Dutch discover that played an important role in advancing the Scientific Revolution? (p. 442)

REVIEW AND ANTICIPATION

1.   Think about the policies of the absolute monarchs like Louis XIV of France. Were the policies of the early Stuart monarchs consistent with what they observed elsewhere in Europe?

2.   Review the religious beliefs and political policies of Philip II. How do you think his policies affected the form of government that was established in the Netherlands?

3.   Which of these countries, Great Britain or the Netherlands, do you think will be able to continue its leadership role? Why?

Chapter 34
Overseas Colonization
and the Competition for Empire

OVERVIEW

After the initial explorations of the Spanish and the Portuguese, many other European countries got involved in the struggle for trade and colonies all over the world. European culture left a profound impact on peoples in the New World as well as in Africa and the Far East.

1.   The New World: The English, the French, and the Dutch. Since Spain and Portugal had established their dominance early in South America, England, France and the Netherlands focused their colonizing efforts on North America and the Caribbean. The English were the most successful, and were able to seize the Dutch and French colonies in the seventeenth and eighteenth centuries.

2.   European Penetration of the Far East and Africa. The English, French, and Dutch actively established trading colonies to profit from the valuable trade with the East. The colonies in India and Africa were primarily trading not settlement colonies. The lucrative slave trade affected Africa far inland from the coastal trading colonies.

3.   The Impact of European Expansion: Native Americans. When the Europeans arrived in the New World, they came with the expectation of making a profit from the plantation system or settling lands. Both motives caused severe disruptions in and exploitation of the native populations.

4.   The Impact of European Expansion: The Far East. Europeans traveling to the Far East found highly developed civilizations resistant to European influence. India had a strong society ruled by Moslem Moguls with long-standing traditions and a strong caste system. Europeans established trading colonies on the coast to take advantage of trade. China, too, had a strong civilization ruled by the Manchu dynasty, and Japan under the shoguns felt so self-sufficient that they excluded Europeans from all access to Japan.

5.   The Impact of European Expansion: Sub-Saharan Africa. Contact with Europeans disrupted much of sub-Saharan Africa, from the highly developed Moslem-influenced states to the native populations in the interior. Europeans looking for gold and especially slaves plundered Africa's human resources, contributing nothing in return.

6.   The Struggle for Overseas Empire. The establishment of overseas empires
        caused European rivalries to take on a global scale. In addition, global
        economics and the politics of mercantilism further stimulated competition and
        struggle for empire. These motives led to a number of wars during the
        seventeenth and eighteenth centuries.

MAP EXERCISE

1.   Locate the following: Russia, China, India, Philippines, Africa, South
        America, Mexico, Great Britain, Portugal, Spain, Ottoman Empire.

2.   Mark the major colonies of each of the following European countries: Spain,
        Portugal, Great Britain, France, and Russia.

3.   Look at the distances as shown by the mileage key. Which colonies were the
        closest to the European powers? Which were the farthest? How far was it
        from Russia to its North American colony?

4.   How far was it from Spain to its colony in the Philippines? Why was it
        worth holding such a small colony so far from Europe?

STUDY QUESTIONS

1.   What policies did the governments of Britain, France and the Netherlands
        pursue with regard to their colonies? How did the differing approaches allow
        England to become the most successful of these three colonizers?

2.   In what regions did the Dutch and British establish trading colonies in the
        Far East and Africa? What role did trading companies play in the colonizing
        efforts? How much impact did the Europeans have in these areas? Why?

3.   Describe the relationship between the European settlers and the native
        American populations. What were the differences between the way the
        Spanish and Portuguese, English and French settlers treated the native
        peoples? Which resulted in the worst consequences for the Indians?

4.   Why was the European impact on the native populations in the Far East so
        much less than in the New World?

5.   What system of governments did Europeans find in India, China, and Japan?
        What impact did the Europeans have on these governments?

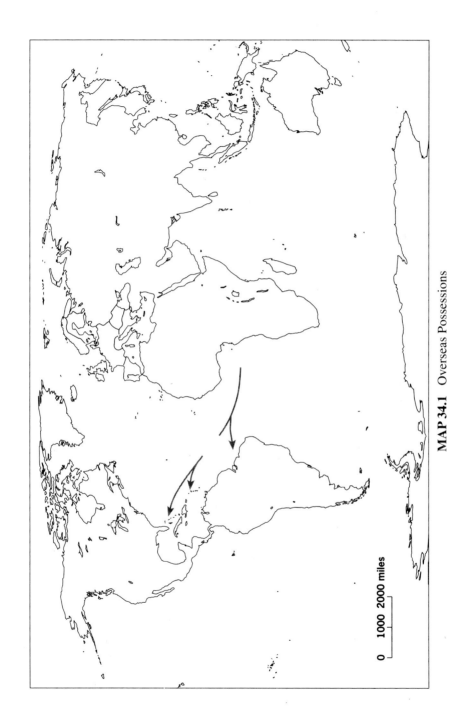

MAP 34.1 Overseas Possessions

6.   What was the European impact on sub-Saharan Africa? How was the impact different between the regions of Moslem influence and those of the interior?

7.   Describe the slave trade and how it influenced the political and social life of Africa. What states were wealthy before 1500, and which rose to prominence as a result of the slave trade?

8.   What economic policies contributed to the European struggle for overseas empires? What wars were fought over the domination of territories outside of Europe? What country emerged as the main victor of these struggles?

IDENTIFICATION

TRY TO USE EACH OF THESE TERMS AT LEAST ONCE IN ANSWERING THE STUDY QUESTIONS AND MAP EXERCISES

Cape of Good Hope	Mogul	Brahmin
Manchu	Asante	Ghana
Ngola	mercantilism	King William's War
War of Spanish	Queen Anne's War	King George's War
Succession	War of Austrian	French & Indian War
Seven Years' War	Succession	William Pitt
	Robert Clive	

SAMPLE QUESTIONS

1.   In what areas of the New World did the English, French, and Dutch focus their colonizing efforts? (pp. 446-447)

2.   What was the major economic activity in the French colonies of the West Indies? (p. 446)

3.   What commodities from the Indies did the Dutch successfully market to European countries? (p. 448)

4.   The Spanish and Portuguese viewed the Indians solely for what purpose? (p. 450)

5.   In what region of the New World did enough American Indian culture survive to give society a special hybrid character? (p. 450)

6.   What was the main reason that Europeans were unable to make much of an impact in the Far East during the seventeenth and eighteenth centuries? (p. 451)

7. What was the dynasty that ruled China in the seventeenth century? (p. 451)

8. A number of sub-saharan African states grew very prosperous prior to 1500. What brought these states their prosperity? (p. 452)

9. What was the economic system of the southern African populations outside the sphere of Moslem influence? (p. 452)

10. What did the Navigation Act of 1651 require? (p. 454)

11. What economic system centers on maintaining a favorable balance of gold and silver coming into the economy? (p. 454)

12. What did the Treaty of Paris accomplish? (p. 455)

REVIEW AND ANTICIPATION

1. Review the areas of Spanish and Portuguese exploration. Where did this force England, France and the Netherlands to focus their attention? Which areas do you think turned out to be most profitable in the long run?

2. Think about the chapter on absolute monarchies and the ways in which absolute monarchs worked to increase their power. Are the explorations and the economic policies described in this chapter consistent with those policies?

3. Do you think Europeans will be content to stay largely excluded from trade with China and Japan? What will motivate them to push for more access to those countries?

4. Which areas of the world do you think will have the most difficult time recovering from the effects of European colonization? Why?

Chapter 35
The Scientific Revolution

OVERVIEW

Beginning in the sixteenth century, there were new ideas and discoveries that profoundly changed the way people viewed the universe and themselves. These ideas transformed thought and society.

1. Causes and Spread. The causes of the Scientific Revolution extend back well before the sixteenth century. The ideas of the Renaissance and, less importantly, of the Reformation forwarded the search for new ideas. In addition, the printing press facilitated the spread of new concepts. Finally, seventeenth-century governments supported new discoveries as a way to increase their own power.

2. Astronomy and Physics: From Copernicus to Newton. A series of great thinkers from the sixteenth through the eighteenth centuries slowly built upon each other's discoveries to begin to understand the structure of the physical universe. They established that the sun was the center of the solar system, and studied the principles of motion that governed planetary movement. Finally, they could explain the universe by a series of mathematical laws.

3. Scientific Methodology. In addition to new discoveries, the new science featured new methodology that emphasized skepticism, experimentation, and reasoning based on observation and mathematics. Two of the main proponents of this new methodology were Francis Bacon and René Descartes.

4. Other Disciplines. The methods of the Scientific Revolution were applied to many other fields, including medicine, anatomy, chemistry, mathematics, and political theory, transforming those disciplines.

5. Impact. While the end of the seventeenth century saw the replacement of the medieval Aristotelian world view with the Copernican-Newtonian universe, the ideas and discoveries affected only a few people, and these were mostly men.

STUDY QUESTIONS

1. What was the view of the universe that had prevailed before the Scientific Revolution? What things facilitated the breakdown of that view and its replacement with a new scientific view?

2.   Describe the series of discoveries in astronomy and physics from the sixteenth through the eighteenth centuries that led to the acceptance of a heliocentric universe that was governed by mathematical laws. Be sure to include the major figures involved in these discoveries.

3.   Describe the scientific method. What skills does it advocate? What were the contributions of the main proponents of the new method? Do we still emphasize this method today?

4.   How was the scientific method applied to the disciplines of anatomy and chemistry in the sixteenth and seventeenth centuries? What were the main discoveries (include both theory and technology)? Which of these discoveries has the most impact today?

5.   What were the significant developments in mathematics? Why was the study of mathematics so central to the scientific enterprise?

6.   What two political philosophers of the seventeenth century applied the scientific method to political theory? What were their main ideas? Which political theorist comes closest to our views of human nature and governance?

7.   What was the impact of the Scientific Revolution on women in the seventeenth century? What women scientists were involved, and why weren't there more women represented? Are women still underrepresented today?

8.   What was the impact of the Scientific Revolution on the masses of people?

IDENTIFICATION

TRY TO USE EACH OF THESE TERMS AT LEAST ONCE IN ANSWERING THE STUDY QUESTIONS

*Aristotle	*Ptolemy	*Nicolaus Copernicus
*Tycho Brahe	*Johann Kepler	
heliocentric	*Galileo Galilei	*Isaac Newton
Francis Bacon	René Descartes	Vesalius
William Harvey	Robert Boyle	Sir John Napier
logarithms	William Leibnitz	Leeuwenhoek
Leviathan	Thomas Hobbes	John Locke
	Margaret Cavendish	Sibylla Merian

CHRONOLOGY

List in chronological order the words in the Identification section that have an asterisk (*). As you list these items, put a circle around those that are contemporary.

SAMPLE QUESTIONS

1.   What were two scientific academies that were established by governments to advance scientific discoveries? (p. 459)

2.   What is the central idea of the view of the world known as the Copernican revolution? (p. 459)

3.   Which scientist had his views on the nature of the universe condemned by the Inquisition in 1633? (p. 461)

4.   Who wrote *Dialogue on the Two Chief Systems of the World* which popularized scientific discoveries? (p. 461)

5.   Who wrote *Principia* or *The Mathematical Principles of Natural Knowledge* which explained the laws of motion in the universe? (p. 461)

6.   Who discovered analytic geometry? (p. 462)

7.   What is "Cartesian dualism"? (p. 463)

8.   Who are regarded as the founders of the science of anatomy? (p. 463)

9.   Who laid the foundations for modern chemistry and discovered a law of gases? (p. 463)

10.   What is the language in which science is expressed? (p. 463)

11.   What political theorist justified absolutism in the name of law and order? (p. 464)

12.   What political theorist concluded that British constitutionalism was in accordance with natural law? (p. 464)

REVIEW AND ANTICIPATION

1.   Review the characteristics of Renaissance and humanist thought, and decide which ones would have been most important in forwarding scientific thought.

2.   How do you think the scientific method and way of viewing the world will influence other aspects of society? Will it have an impact on social life, or economics, or other disciplines? How?

3.   What do you think is the most important reason for people to adopt new scientific ideas?

Chapter 36
The Enlightenment

OVERVIEW

During the eighteenth century, a new way of thinking that had been influenced by the Scientific Revolution swept through European society, making an impact on all aspects of life and thought including everything from politics to economics to society.

1.   Enlightenment Concepts. Enlightenment thinkers stressed three concepts in formulating their thought: 1) belief in the power of reason to solve problems in all fields; 2) belief that nature is rational, good, and governed by laws; and 3) belief in the value of change and progress. Enlightenment thinkers used these concepts to criticize institutions and customs of the past (including religious structures) in the hopes of bringing about a new era of freedom and reason.

2.   The *Philosophes*. Proponents of Enlightenment thought were known in France as *philosophes* (the French word for "philosopher"). These people were usually not formally trained nor associated with universities, but were interested in the new scientific ideas as well as literary products of the age. Their broad tastes are reflected in the publication of the *Encyclopedia*, which summarized knowledge from their perspective. *Philosophes* were influenced by Isaac Newton, John Locke and other giants of the Scientific Revolution. The greatest French *philosophe* was Voltaire, although others, like Adam Smith and Jean-Jacques Rousseau, were equally influential.

3.   Women and the Social Context. Women contributed to the growth of Enlightenment thought by serving as patrons of gatherings in the salons of Paris in which thinkers were brought together to exchange ideas. Women also contributed money to some *philosophes*. While Enlightenment thinkers generally supported improved education for women, they did not advocate equal rights for women.

4.   Enlightenment and Religion. Enlightenment thinkers generally were in conflict with Christian churches in their view that an impersonal God was rational and had set the universe in motion, never to tamper with it again. As part of their rational approach, *philosophes* did advocate toleration of religious minorities (like Jews).

5.   Political and Economic Aspects of the Enlightenment. Enlightenment thinkers turned their attention to discovering the most efficient and benevolent political and economic institutions. Influential political thinkers like Locke,

Montesquieu, and Rousseau wrote treatises that exerted profound influence on developing governments, and economists like Adam Smith developed *laissez faire* economic principles that continue to shape the modern world.

6. Enlightened Despotism. Instead of believing in revolution to bring about Enlightenment thought, many *philosophes* believed that enlightened despotism would be the best way to introduce reform. Several absolute rulers in Europe believed themselves to be shaped by enlightened thought and attempted to introduce such reforms. Since these rulers represented entrenched authority, most of their reforms were superficial.

7. Conclusion. The Enlightenment introduced a way of thinking into Europe that had a profound and lasting impact well into the modern times.

STUDY QUESTIONS

1. Describe the main ideas of the Enlightenment *philosophes* and tell how these ideas were expressed by the greatest Enlightenment figures. What did they attack, and what did they support?

2. What contribution did women make to the growth of French Enlightenment thought?

3. What was the Enlightenment's view of religion? Include in your discussion their position on the nature of God and on the treatment of religious minorities.

4. Who were the three greatest Enlightenment political thinkers, and what was the major contribution of each to political philosophy?

5. Who was the greatest Enlightenment economist, and what was his philosophy? What economic philosophy did the enlightened despot Frederick the Great adhere to? Was that consistent with his other Enlightenment policies? Why do you think he advocated that position?

6. Who were the enlightened despots, and what reforms did they attempt to introduce in their countries? How successful were they? Why?

IDENTIFICATION

TRY TO USE EACH OF THESE TERMS AT LEAST ONCE IN ANSWERING THE STUDY QUESTIONS

philosophes   Voltaire   D. Diderot

Adam Smith	J-J Rousseau	M. Wollstonecraft
deism	John Locke	Montesquieu
The Spirit of the Laws	*Social Contract*	*Wealth of Nations*
Two Treatises of Civil	Physiocrats	*laissez faire*
Government	Frederick the Great	Joseph II
	Catherine the Great	

SAMPLE QUESTIONS

1.   How did Enlightenment thinkers view human beings? (p. 467)

2.   What were the three most important concepts that characterized Enlightenment thought? (p. 467)

3.   Who was the great synthesizer of the Scientific Revolution who influenced the *philosophes*? (p. 468)

4.   What publication sold popularly and served to spread the ideas of the Enlightenment outside the major cities? (pp. 469-471)

5.   In the primary document, "The Philosophe," the author writes, "Reason is in the estimation of the Philosopher what grace is to the Christian." What does he mean by that? (p. 470)

6.   How did the ideas of Rousseau differ from those of most of the *philosophes*? (p. 471)

7.   In what way(s) did most of the *philosophes* support improving the rights of women? (p. 472)

8.   What was the major difference between *philosophes*' view of the role of God in the universe and that of Christian churches? (p. 472)

9.   What are the natural rights of human beings according to Locke? (p. 473)

10.   According to Locke, if a government interferes with an individual's private ownership of property, what rights and responsibilities does that individual have? (p. 473)

11.   Who was influential in developing the idea of a system of checks and balances in government? (p. 473)

12.   What is *laissez faire* economics? (pp. 473-474)

13.   What does "enlightened despotism" mean? (p. 474)

14.   What reforms did enlightened rulers attempt to introduce? (p. 474)

REVIEW AND ANTICIPATION

1.   How do the concepts of the Enlightenment resemble the ideas of the Scientific Revolution? How do these ideas contrast with those of the Renaissance and the Middle Ages?

2.   How do the religious ideas of the Enlightenment contrast with those of the Reformation? In thinking ahead to the American Revolution, which of these ideas will most influence the Founding Fathers?

3.   Which of the ideas of the Enlightenment political and economic thinkers do you think will have the most profound effect in the American and subsequent revolutions?

4.   What do you think will be the most effective way for societies to adopt enlightened ideas? (Revolution? Despotism? Some other way?)

5.   In the "Retrospect" section, the author summarizes the events from the Renaissance through the Enlightenment. Which of these events do you think were most important in shaping Enlightenment thought?